FRENCH CHURCH ARCHITECTURE

FRENCH CHURCH ARCHITECTURE

BY
E. TYRRELL-GREEN

LONDON
THE SHELDON PRESS
NORTHUMBERLAND AVENUE, W.C.2
NEW YORK AND TORONTO: THE MACMILLAN CO.

First published 1928

Printed in Great Britain

TO

MY FRIENDS IN FRANCE

EMMELINE AND ISABELLE HATTERSLEY

OF PAU AND GUÉTHARY

AND

TROUP HOWARD MATHEWS

OF STE.-ADRESSE

THIS BOOK

IS

AFFECTIONATELY DEDICATED

O séculaires Basiliques
Que la foi de vieux temps fonda
Chantez en accents symboliques
L'universel Sursum Corda.

I stood before the triple northern port,
Where dedicated shapes of saints and kings,
Stern faces bleared with immemorial watch,
Looked down benignly grave and seemed to say,
" Ye come and go incessant ; we remain
Safe in the hallowed quiets of the past :
Be reverent, ye who flit and are forgot,
Of faith so nobly realised as this."

J. Russell Lowell : *The Cathedral* (Chartres).

PREFACE

UNTIL recent years the greater part of France was almost unknown to the average traveller, for its exploration was a somewhat difficult and tedious process, involving irksome waiting for local trains and the finding of chance vehicles at country stations. The advent of the bicycle and then of the motor-car, together with the enterprise of the great French railways, the P.O. and the P.L.M., in organising motor-tours, have opened up the provinces of France to the tourist as never before, so that on French roads and in French towns British and American visitors have become expected and welcome guests.

The pleasure of touring in France is complex. There is, of course, the charm of climate and atmosphere. The air—away from the coast—is singularly dry, so that, powerful as the sun's rays may be, excessive heat is obviated, the landscape is clear, and the distances, unshrouded by mist, succeed one another in delicate outlines. Of scenery there is endless variety and large regions are wildly picturesque—the rocky coast of Brittany, the passes of the Pyrenees and Alps, the gorges of the Tarn, the wide sweep of majestic rivers or the fantastic outlines of the volcanic region of Auvergne, while their strange character imparts a fascination of their own to the *Landes* of the south-west, or to the *Camargue* and the *Crau* of the Mediterranean coast.

Art adds to what nature has given. Natural scenery

owes much of its impressiveness and its attraction for us to architecture. How would the heights of Coutances or of Laon be specially attractive without their diadem of towers? It is not the background of mountains merely, or the rich and varied vegetation that makes the charm of the valley of the Rhône, but the extraordinarily picturesque towns upon its banks and the castles perched on every hill-top. The mention of the Loire calls up visions of the stately *châteaux* of Touraine, and the rugged scenery of Velay has its interest increased tenfold by church or fortress crowning many a needle-like rock. Scenes otherwise tame and commonplace are for us full of charm through the presence of works of architecture, and in those parts of France where there are no forests or mountains on a grand scale her buildings are most beautiful. From out the dead level of the waving cornfields of *La Beauce* the celestial fane of Chartres rears her twin spires. The fragment of Beauvais rises like a gigantic cliff from a sea of meadows. Noyon broods like a heavenly dove over the Oise. Bourges with its interminable nave adorns a portion of the centre of France which, without it and its delightful city that clusters around it, would have little attraction. Chaucer's reference in the Clerk's tale is very true of France—

> A lusty plain abundant of vitaille,
> Where many a toun and tower thou mayest behold
> That founded were in time of fadres olde,
> And many another delitable sight.

To say that France is a land of Architecture is to repeat what everyone knows. But there are surprisingly few people who have any adequate idea of the wealth and splendour of her architectural possessions. It is in the old province of Transalpine Gaul, now Southern France, that we are best able to reconstruct for ourselves the life of ancient Rome, for the historic monuments exhibit the style of Imperial Rome unchanged. Not even Rome herself can show any remains of a theatre fit to be compared with those of Nîmes and Arles. She has no temple remaining nearly so perfect as the Maison Carrée of Nîmes, nor does she possess an aqueduct equal to the Pont-du-Gard. The Architecture of France was derived at the outset from Imperial Rome, and she borrowed again from Italy the revived Roman of the Renaissance. In other stages of her Architectural History her development has been her own very vigorous work. She took the common Romanesque architecture extant in the tenth century and gave it many different plies. The Norman phase of it she carried into Britain and we know it well in England. But there are equally interesting fashions of Romanesque building, each with its own peculiar characteristics, belonging to Burgundy, Auvergne, Aquitaine and Saintonge, which have to be studied on their native soil. The pointed style to which the name of Gothic has been given we have in England, but it was in France that it took its rise, and it is in that country that one has to look for its most stupendous works. Then when the Middle Ages had ended, the Renaissance covered France afresh with architectural splendour as individual and national as Renaissance work can ever be.

This book has been undertaken by one who loves France and knows her well—her highways and byways, busy centres and remote country districts—in the hope that it may serve as a guide to the better appreciation of her architectural treasures by the ever-increasing number of English-speaking tourists. The writer's aim has been to tell the traveller who is interested in old churches, though, maybe, without technical knowledge of architecture, what to see in the places he may visit and how to appreciate that which he sees. At the same time the student of Architecture may find in the book a useful introduction to its subject, a handy work of reference and a convenient summary and guide to the study of French churches.

E. T.-G.

Bayonne, 1927.

ACKNOWLEDGMENTS

The treatment of French Church Architecture in the following pages is the outcome of my own study and observation during some periods of residence in France and in the course of tours planned for the study of her ancient churches. The comparatively full treatment of churches in the Limousin, Cantal and Auvergne is due to the appeal which that part of France, little visited by English tourists, makes to me through associations with my mother's family, the Dores of Auvergne.

I have found Brossard's *Géographie Pittoresque et Monumentale de la France* in five volumes by Flammarion (Paris, 1900) of the greatest value as a guide to architectural monuments, and have been constantly indebted to it, as well as to the beautiful publication *Le Pays de France* in three volumes by Hachette (Paris, 1925). Three little books by Broquelet entitled *Nos Églises, Nos Abbayes,* and *Nos Cathédrales* have been my companions on ecclesiological journeys. Of works in English I have been chiefly indebted to Professor E. A. Freeman's *Sketches from French Travel* and *Sketches of Travel in Normandy and Maine,* both models of the treatment of architecture in relation to history, and to the Rev. H. H. Bishop's *Pictorial Architecture of France* (S.P.C.K.). This last attracted my interest especially to some famous Burgundian churches, and, in particular, I have adopted the author's suggestion with regard to the unique plan of the west end of the Cathedral of Le Puy. The MS. notes and library of the late Rev. William Ashe, formerly chaplain at Caen, which were generously handed over to me before his death have proved invaluable for the understanding of the churches of Normandy and Brittany, and of this collection the works of the great French ecclesiologist de Caumont have been indispensable.

The line illustrations in the text are from my own sketches, many of them made in view of this book, but the drawings on pages 93, 95, 120, 132, 138, 163, 164, 166, 167, 168, 170, 171, 172, 181, 182, 192, 195, 230, 234, 235, 236 and 237 appeared in my book *Towers and Spires*, and to the publishers, Messrs. Wells Gardner, Darton & Co., my thanks are due for allowing their reproduction in the present work. I would also gratefully acknowledge the courtesy of those who have permitted the use of their photographs for illustrations, the source of which is indicated in each case.

E. T.-G.

CONTENTS

CHAPTER I

OUTSTANDING FEATURES OF FRENCH CHURCH ARCHITECTURE

CHAPTER II

ROMANESQUE—ITS ORIGINS

CHAPTER III

ROMANESQUE—ITS FURTHER LOCAL VARIETIES

CHAPTER IV

ROMANESQUE—ITS DETAILS

CHAPTER V

GOTHIC—ITS RISE AND DEVELOPMENT

CHAPTER VI

GOTHIC—ITS DETAILS

CHAPTER VII

RENAISSANCE

CHAPTER VIII

ON SOME SPECIAL CLASSES OF STRUCTURE

LIST OF ILLUSTRATIONS

FRENCH CHURCH ARCHITECTURE

CHAPTER I

OUTSTANDING FEATURES OF FRENCH CHURCH ARCHITECTURE

1. The French a Building People

The French are not only an architectural people but a building people as well. Every town and village—we may almost add every farmhouse—witnesses to the national delight in piling up great masses of stone. The English, except during the Norman period, were not a building people. They instinctively save material where the Frenchman's impulse is to lavish it, and this impulse has greatly added to the interest and charm of his country. The much greater size, height and solidity of even ordinary buildings in French towns and villages is one of the contrasts which most impress and interest the traveller in rural as in urban France. The French accordingly are not at their best when attempting anything small or simple which has to take its place in a country landscape. Theirs has been, for the most part, an art which aims at the placing of monumental works amongst the dwellings of the people. The greatest of these works are their churches. But it must not be inferred that the French country church is inferior in beauty or interest, as a rule, to an English parish church. In England parish churches form rather a class by themselves, whereas in France there is not the same clearly marked distinction between the cathedral or minster and the parochial type. There the soaring vault, the clustered chapels, the great *rosaçe* and the deeply-recessed portal of the cathedral were reproduced in the parochial church. Thus France has parish churches which are not excelled elsewhere either in beauty or interest. There are no finer examples of "Norman" or of early Pointed work than in the village churches of Normandy, especially in the neighbourhood of Caen and Bayeux. The churches of the Department of the Oise in the district about Senlis and Creil exhibit Gothic in its perfection and there is scarcely a parallel elsewhere to the wonderful domed churches of the Charente with their richly adorned portals in a Romanesque style which exhibits a marked Byzantine influence.

2. The Churches of France

No one can know France unless he knows her churches. They breathe a life more intimate than her rivers or her hills, for there is a soul in the stones of which ancient cities are compounded, and that soul is more nobly expressed in the churches than elsewhere. In old time the châteaux, the civic halls, the ramparts shared with cathedrals and churches this appealing solemnity. They were all of them symbols of the vigour of manifold human activity. But time has weighed heavily upon the palaces, the fortresses and the girdle of ramparts. They have had to make way for fresh developments of civilisation and have left but their ruins behind them or are artificially preserved like specimens in a museum. Ruins and specimens are curiosities and may be very interesting, but they are dead, even the best preserved of them, like the *Cité* of Carcassonne. It is in the churches of France alone that the old life still lives. As we enter and the leathern *portière* closes behind us our eyes get accustomed to the dim light to find that here at least the old inspiration is intensely alive. For within there seems to centre still the spirit and powerful personality of a land where the joys and experiences of to-day are curiously mingled with vivid memories of a romantic and poignant past, because architecture is the most sensitive of all the arts, responding to the play of human thought, and registering the life of the people that produces it.

3. The Appeal of Size

From what has been already said with reference to the French as a building people it follows that their architecture has the power and the mighty appeal that size can give, for this in itself, apart from other considerations, is sufficient to ensure a general admiration. The traveller in France soon realises that he is in a large land, with buildings on a correspondingly great scale, and it is in their wonderfully impressive height that they especially excel. As the Gothic style advanced, the vaults of great French churches soared ever higher. The cathedral of Reims rises to 125 feet while Amiens exceeds it by another 15 feet, and the aspiration of the Gothic builders of the North culminates in the choir of Beauvais, where the bosses of the vaults are 156 feet above the pavement. A comparison with English Gothic churches is instructive, for the height of the nave of Salisbury Cathedral is but 84 feet, while even the French-looking Abbey of Westminster does not exceed 104 feet. This natural tendency of skilful architects to build high, led to some important consequences as regards the general aspect of a church. In the first place the relatively short transept is characteristic of the French churches, and is æsthetically right, considering that in proportion to their height the churches themselves are short in comparison with English ones. The longer churches with less height could well bear long transepts, like the English cathedrals or the great Abbey of Cluny or St.-Sernin Toulouse. With the astonishing upward growth of the great French Gothic churches the transepts were naturally shortened, or, as at Nantes and Bourges, omitted altogether. The lofty French churches could only bear transepts shorter than the English ones, and but a single transept—not double as at Canterbury, York and Lincoln—if any at all. But the effect of height and mass on the exterior was not only increased by the shortening of the transepts, it was still further enhanced by the fact that the intended groups of towers were found incompatible, beyond a certain limit, with other developments. Of the seven towers of Rouen three only are reared above the ridge of the roof, while at Laon the like number—seven—stand in confused assemblage in various stages of completion. Chartres and Reims appear as two-towered churches, whereas nine were intended in each case, and once the stature of Reims was exceeded the tower-clusters disappear. The two at Amiens scarcely rise above the mass of the cathedral in a distant view, practically forming a sort of screen-façade at the west end of the church, and neither there nor at Beauvais were towers designed to flank the transept ends. From certain points of view, indeed, some of the great Gothic churches of France have the appearance of towers themselves, an appearance enhanced by the fact that owing to the daring and ambitious scale on which they were designed, especially to their excesssive height, they have never been completed. So do the choir of Beauvais and the nave of St.-Wulfran at Abbeville soar above the houses beneath.

4. The Appeal of Gloom

While the great scale of French churches is one of the factors which go to produce the effect they have upon us, even a casual visitor will be awed by many French interiors, and impressed by the solemnity of their gloom. There may be some who feel the inconsistency of "dim religious light," and who would allow no darkness in a house consecrated to Him who is Light. Yet surely the devout and sincere spirit feels not only the glory and triumph of the Cross, but also the darkness that overshadowed it, and there is a deep meaning in the symbolism of the sanctuary, which suggests that all things are not yet made manifest but there is still place for dimness and mystery in earthly temples. Upon entering there falls upon the spirit a certain awe, a vague appreciation that in the life we lead there is some great lack, which within these walls might be supplied had we the power to grasp it. To this feeling everything seems to contribute, the lofty pillars above which the spring of the vault is half revealed, the jewel-like flashes from stained windows, the placid images of the Saints, the faint glimmer of votive candles, the steady point of light burning before one altar, the lingering scent of incense, the motionless figures kneeling here and there—all these things have their effect upon us. But however this may be, there can be no sort of doubt as to the value of gloom and mysterious shadow as an element of architectural effect. Almost every interior gains immensely in architectural sublimity as the darkness deepens and the shadows gather within. Many a great French interior —Albi, Bourges, Notre-Dame de Paris—will seem as the shadow of a great rock in a weary land, and amongst the most abiding and thrilling memories of a lifetime will be that of entering the cathedral of Chartres at dusk.

One poet has sung "of Milan the gloom and the glory," and Barcelona Cathedral has been called "the cathedral of the Night," and its interior is the most moving and awe-inspiring in the world just because the dim religious light of which another poet wrote is there at its holiest and most grave.

5. Unity

Whether we consider a building belonging to one of the types of Romanesque, or a Gothic church, there is about these structures in France a much more notable unity of design than is at all common in English churches. The great French Romanesque churches have each been planned as a coherent whole, and in comparatively few instances has the design been overlaid or obscured by later additions in a divergent architectural style. Thus exceptional are such cases as St.-Amable, Riom (Puy de Dôme), where the choir of a church of typical Auvergnat Romanesque has been rebuilt in Gothic, or Notre-Dame d'Avénières Laval (Mayenne), where a church of Angevin Romanesque has received a central tower and spire of the very latest Flamboyant style with a touch of Renaissance about it. There is a like impressive unity about the Gothic churches of the North. This is partly due to the fact that there was a much more strongly marked uniformity in Gothic buildings in France from the twelfth to the fourteenth century than was the case in England. Thus there is to be observed a progressive relation between the cathedrals of Noyon, Paris, Soissons, Reims and Amiens, indicating a common and co-ordinated influence which it would be difficult to parallel in kindred groups elsewhere. Besides this there is an individual unity and coherence of design in such churches, the like of which is rare in Britain. French architects always seem to have set greater store by unity than the less logical English builders. Even when the creation of a great church was spread over a long period they were careful to preserve unity of conception and design, avoiding as a rule those contrasts of style which we not only tolerate but even admire as giving some added interest to English churches.

6. Lofty Late Gothic Chancels

There is, however, one particular way in which this distinctive unity is not infrequently lacking, owing to the fact that a great scheme for rebuilding a church during the prevalence of the Gothic style was arrested before it could attain completion. Such rebuilding or alteration was commmenced in the choir, but, from one cause or another, never carried out in the nave. Thus we fairly often, in France, meet with a very lofty choir—or choir and transepts—joined to a very much lower and humble-looking nave. In this way the outline of many a church forms the greatest possible contrast to what we are accustomed to in England, where the chancel roof is almost always on a lower level than that of the nave. Beauvais Cathedral shows the most marked and exaggerated instance of this arrested development, where the loftiest of all Gothic choirs dwarfs into entire insignificance a Romanesque nave which may be as early as the sixth century. The fine Romanesque nave of St.-Étienne in the same city has a later Gothic choir with very tall clerestory windows, its greater height extending to the west of the transept crossing. The late and ornate chancel of St.-Antoine Compiègne, similarly dwarfs the rest of the church, and in the same department of *Oise* other examples may be noted at Cires-les-Mello and in the little village church of Sérifontaine. Le Mans Cathedral, like Beauvais, has its lofty choir and transepts towering above an earlier nave, and we constantly come across instances—St.-Étienne Elbœuf (Seine-Inférieure) is a striking one ; Exmes and Écouché (Orne) have lofty Flamboyant choirs attached to low and spreading naves ; Redon (Ille-et-Vilaine), Norrey (Calvados), Beaumont-le-Roger and Conches (Eure), St.-Jean Troyes (Aube), Evron (Mayenne) may be added to the list as notable cases. Ibos (Htes.-Pyrénées) and St.-Thibault (Côte d'Or) have in each case a chancel so lofty as to appear at a little distance like a fine tower, while at Tonnerre (Yonne) are churches with extremely lofty chancels joined to low naves. Farther west Suèvres (Loir-et-Cher) near the Loire has a flèche between its long nave and the loftier chancel and apse.

7. The Planning of the East End, with Apse and Radiating Chapels

Besides the above-noted characteristics which belong to the general aspect of French churches, there are also some very distinctive features belonging rather to the details of planning or design. First of these should be mentioned the fondness of the French builders for the apse at the east end with its ambulatory, or circumscribing aisle, and radiating chapels. This arrangement, found alike in Romanesque and in Gothic churches in France, forms the greatest possible contrast to the rectangular and—except in cathedrals, collegiate churches and buildings of the Perpendicular style—usually aisleless chancels of the English churches.

The apse is one of those features of the plan of a Christian church derived from the basilicas of ancient Rome and in the earliest examples of its adaptation was at the west end, the priest taking the eastward position and facing the congregation across the altar. Into this country the apse came with the introduction of Christianity into Roman Britain, and an interesting example of it has come to light by the discovery at the close of the last century of the basilica at Silchester (Hants) with the apse at the west end in the ancient fashion. In France the cathedral of Nevers shows this arrangement. Its western apse is Romanesque, and the church has at a later period been turned round, as it were, by the erection of a Gothic apse in what had become the usual place at the east end. There is another example of this planning in France in the village church of Echinghen (Pas-de-Calais). Here in the west wall are some remains of a round tower communicating with the apse. The whole building is of early Romanesque, and old plans show that there was an analogous apse at the opposite end of the church. Thus it would seem that Echinghen is one of the very few churches in France with an eastern and western apse.[1]

Having first come to England with the introduction of Christianity under the Romans the apse was afterwards repeatedly brought into this country by influence from the Continent. Through the mission of St. Augustine it was planted at Canterbury, but in the country generally the Celtic fashion of building churches with a square east end prevailed over it. Then with the Conquest by Duke William came the great apse of the Norman builders, and we see it at Canterbury and in the great minsters at Norwich, Peterborough and Tewkesbury. Yet how soon the Anglo-Norman builders abandoned

[1] The western apse was more often retained in Germany, especially in the Rhineland, where churches were built in the Romanesque style with an apse at either end as in the cathedrals of Trier, Mainz and Worms and the Apostles' church at Cologne. Affinity with Germany is still further shown at Nevers Cathedral by its western apse roof being hipped at the north and south, instead of terminating in the usual gables. Langford (Essex) afforded an example of an English church with two apses, probably of the eleventh century, but a later extension of the building eastward swallowed up the eastern apse.

the apse may be seen in the fine cruciform church, with rectangular east end, raised by Henry of Blois, brother of King Stephen and Bishop of Winchester, for the Hospital of St. Cross near his cathedral city. Not only in England, moreover, but across the Channel in the Romanesque and early Pointed styles of our Norman and Plantaganet Kings we frequently meet with the rectangular chancel.[1] After the culminating examples at Reims, Amiens and Beauvais the apse was taken over almost everywhere where the Gothic style overflowed from its home in France, from Prague to Toledo. It came again to England in the Royal Abbey of Westminster in the time of Henry III. But the apse never really took root in this country, and the typical English church, cathedral or parochial, is square-ended towards the east.[2]

On the other hand, in France, Romanesque and Gothic churches alike, whether in Normandy as at Caen, in the south as at Toulouse, in Burgundy as at Vézelay, in Poitou as at Poitiers, in Auvergne at Clermont-Ferrand and Issoire, or in the Gothic of the Ile de France—everywhere we meet with the apse, semicircular or polygonal, and its circumscribing aisle with radiating chapels. And in artistic effect there can be no doubt about the superiority of the apse, whether the church be viewed from without or within. There is a wonderful majesty about the east end of a great Romanesque church like St.-Sernin Toulouse, or a typical Auvergnat church such as Issoire, where the tall choir rises above the ambulatory and clustering chapels. Then again in the fully

[1] See below pp. 113–114.

[2] The apse reappears in some late Perpendicular churches of the Midlands, as at St. Michael's Coventry, Aston near Birmingham, Westbury-on-Trym (Gloucs), Witton (Ches.) and the beautiful Savage chapel attached to Macclesfield Parish Church in the same county. Probably the example set in the apsidal east end of Lichfield Cathedral accounts for this late reintroduction of the apse into English Church architecture.

developed Gothic, how much grace as well as firmness there is in the expression of an east end like Amiens, or Orléans where the choir with its spreading aisles and chapels are all linked up by the lace-like flying buttresses. When Notre-Dame de Paris is viewed from the river these buttresses seem to suggest by their form the folded wings of angels kneeling in adoration, and the satisfaction given to the eye by the appearance of solidity was well expressed by R. L. Stevenson when he wrote of the typical east end of a French church as "flanging out in sweeping terraces and settling down broadly upon the earth as though it meant to stay there." Within, as we look towards the high-altar, there cannot be a moment's doubt as to the superiority of the apse, with its aisles and chapels, from the æsthetic point of view. The narrow spacing of the arches in the actual apse is a source of great beauty. The arches across the end of the vista ought to be narrower than those of the side ranges, because the lateral ones, being foreshortened, become greatly narrowed to the eye in a general view, while those directly across present themselves in their actual proportions. The narrower the extreme arches are the greater the beauty. Then there is the great gain of the poetry of pillared aisles and the charm as one moves around the choir, of perspectives varying at every step.

8. Portals and Wealth of Statuary

Another notable feature in which English and French churches differ is in the arrangement of the principal entrances to the building. Grand façades with majestic portals at the west end, and frequently at the transept ends as well, form a striking characteristic of French churches, and in these positions are found the principal entrances not only of cathedrals but also of parish churches. In this country, on the other hand, the usual entrance to a church is through a lateral porch projecting from the nave—most often on the south side—and there is as a rule no attempt at a façade, for the usual fashion of building one tower at the west precluded any such design at that end of the church. Even English cathedrals, when they have a western façade, often adhere to the parochial plan in making a lateral porch the chief means of egress and entrance, as in the Norman minsters at Southwell and Sherborne, or the Gothic cathedrals of Wells and Salisbury. At Canterbury, though there is a large doorway beneath the west window, the chief entrance to the nave is by a lateral porch, to the south of the south-west tower. There are screen façades on a large scale at the west ends of Peterborough, Lincoln and Salisbury cathedrals, but the doorways are in each case much too small in proportion, and at Wells they are absurdly diminutive, suggesting the appearance of mouse-holes in the wainscot of a wall. In France as we enter a cathedral from the north, south or west, we commonly pass beneath cavernous arches surrounded by sculptured figures which help us to realise the cloud of heavenly witnesses, or transport us in spirit where the four-and-twenty elders cast their golden crowns around the crystal sea. The same is true, also, of the western doorway of many a humbler church, for there is no country that can compare with France for splendour of portals. In the days of the early though ornate Romanesque of the south, and in the days of the Gothic splendour of the north alike, France is first and unapproached as regards its portals, with their amazing wealth of exquisite statuary. We feel this as we stand before the west front of St.-Gilles (Gard) or before one of the transept ends of the cathedral of Chartres. At times visions of lovely portals in other lands, of San Marco at Venice or of the golden gate of Santiago de Compostella, may rise before our eyes but only to be dismissed. We are satisfied that in this matter France has not been rivalled in any age. The portals of France take the lead and they are amongst the most glorious of her glorious works.

France is not without fine porches also. We can scarcely count as a porch the splendid western annexe or narthex which we find in the Burgundian Romanesque churches of Vézelay, Autun and Tournus and in the great typical churches of Auvergne—alike designed to carry towers, two in the Burgundian and a single one in the centre of the Auvergnat examples. Large western porches on similar lines occur in the Gothic style at St.-Père-sous-Vézelay (Yonne), Notre-Dame Dijon, Semur-en-Auxois and Beaune (Côte-d'Or) and in the north at Noyon Cathedral. Sometimes porches are formed by the ground-story of a tower which stands on open arches, as at St.-Benoît-sur-Loire (Loiret), Ébreuil (Allier) and Oloron-Ste.-Marie (Basses-Pyrénées), as in England at St. Mary's Warwick. In the latest Gothic style doorways, whether lateral, as at St.-Germain Argentan (Orne) and Valognes (Manche), or western as at St.-Maclou Rouen and Alençon (Orne), have very graceful—in the two last-named lace-like—screens on open archways standing in front of them, in a fashion without parallel in English church architecture. Porches, however, analogous to the usual English ones are comparatively rare. Candes (Indre-et-Loire), Polignac (Haute-Loire), Mello (Oise), Chaumont (Haute-Marne) are instances of Gothic lateral porches in different parts of the land, and to these should be added the lovely porch on the north side at Norrey (Calvados) and the extremely delicate and beautiful south porch at Louviers (Eure). Many a small village church in Normandy has a porch of humble proportions, and the Breton churches of Carnac and St.-Caradec-Trégomel (Morbihan) and

Bar-sur-Aube (Aube).

Pont-Croix (Finistère) have notable lateral porches. Western porches are still less common, but occur at Loches (Indre-et-Loire)—a fine Romanesque example—at Plombières-lès-Dijon (Côte d'Or), Notre-Dame de

Liesse (Aisne), Fismes (Marne), St.-Just (Charente-Inférieure) and Sauveterre-de-Béarn (Basses-Pyrénées). In some cases a porch rests upon pillars and open arches, such as the Romanesque lateral porches at Brioude and Auzon (Haute-Loire) and the very handsome Gothic lateral porches at St.-Urbain Troyes (Aube) and Albi Cathedral (Tarn). A delicately designed early Gothic porch on open arches also projects from the west tower of Bernières (Calvados), and a more curious example of the same class is attached to the west front of Montpellier Cathedral (Hérault). Normandy village churches not uncommonly have wooden porches,[1] and very fine examples of cloister-porches in wood, extending not only across the west end, but also along the side of the church, are found at Bar-sur-Aube (Aube) and Mulsans (Loir-et-Cher).

9. Rose Windows

In one very noticeable detail affecting the shape and tracery of windows there is a marked divergence between French and English taste—viz.: the employment of a large "rose" or "wheel" window. It finds place in no single west front of an English cathedral, though it was allowed to appear in the transept ends of Lincoln and Westminster Abbey and forms the central feature of the east end of Durham as formerly of old St. Paul's. But these are rare cases,[2] whereas in France the *rosaçe* became the rule, scarcely a single typically *French* church being without it. In western Europe two distinct conceptions seem to have been at work as to the most becoming mode of fenestration above the great portal. One was that of using windows of the same kind as those designed

[1] See below, p. 228.

[2] On the distribution of the rose-window in England, see *Parish Church Architecture*, pp. 106–7.

for the rest of the church and arranging them on the façade either singly or in groups. This was the idea that found favour in the Pisan style, in the Rhineland, in Germany, in the Netherlands and in the British Isles. The other type of design employed a great circular window, which naturally became the central feature of the front. This was the favourite conception of Italian builders, as at Siena and Orvieto, and we find it in French architecture in churches of all styles and dates, from the plain circle of the Romanesque at St.-Sernin Toulouse, and the wheels of the more ornate Romanesque at St.-Étienne Beauvais and Trie-Château (Oise), through all the Gothic development when each great French church commonly had three great *rosaçes*—one in the west façade and one in each transept end—as at Chartres, Amiens and Rouen, down to the Renaissance as in the west front of Évreux Cathedral and at St.-Étienne-du-Mont in Paris.[1] Not that this must be understood as implying that the rose-window, while characteristic, is universal in France. It is absent from the fronts of Romanesque churches at Notre-Dame-la-Grande Poitiers, Angoulême Cathedral, the cathedrals of Le Puy and Le Mans, the church of Çivray (Vienne) and the two great Abbeys at Caen. Again, we do not find it in the early pointed style at Pontigny, in the later Gothic of the great churches of Vienne (Isère), Bourges, Tours, Nantes, Coutances, Lisieux, or in the Breton examples at Dol (Ille-et-Vilaine), Tréguier and Dinan (Côtes-du-Nord), Vannes (Morbihan) and Quimper (Finistère). It appears to be the case that the great *rosaçe* which was made so important a feature of the Gothic of the Ile de France spread thence on all sides and became a general favourite, but was less adopted in

[1] On the design of the tracery in rose-windows in France, see below, pp. 150–155.

W. FAÇADE, ST.-GILLES (GARD).

CLOISTER AT ST. TROPHIME, ARLES.

SOUTHERN ROMANESQUE.

facing p. 16.

those provinces where German, Norman, English or Angevin influence was at work.

10. Desecrated Churches

No visitor to France can fail to notice the number of desecrated churches he comes across in the towns, and if he is a student of history he will find also that frequently one or two churches may remain in a town, these being cathedral or collegiate, while many parochial churches in the same place have been destroyed, or maybe a few fragments of them remain. The case of France is very different from that of England in this respect. Each land has passed through its period of destruction, but at different dates and under quite different circumstances and conditions. The suppression of the monasteries in England was an isolated act and did not, at any rate directly, affect the parochial churches. In France, at the Revolution, an attempt was made to suppress everything, the social order as well as all that pertained to religion. Hence in England the ruined churches are, generally speaking, those which belonged to the religious orders alone, the parochial churches remained more or less intact,[1] and in the changes of the sixteenth century the greater churches suffered rather than the small ones. In such towns as Bury St. Edmunds, Coventry, Evesham or Reading the minsters perished, but the parochial churches lived on and are still used for worship. In the French cataclysm of the eighteenth century all churches were suppressed, and when in the nineteenth century some of them were restored to religious uses, it was quite natural that the

[1] Norfolk is an exception to this rule. In that county a large number of parish churches have been wholly or partially ruined, partly through decline of population, and partly through religious indifference and neglect since the days of Queen Elizabeth.

largest buildings and those that were architecturally the finest should be chosen for the purpose. Thus in France we often come across the very opposite state of things to that which obtains in such English towns as those just referred to: the cathedral and the minster remain and are in use, though perhaps shorn of their ecclesiastical status as cathedral or collegiate churches,[1] while the parochial churches have either perished altogether, or, remaining more or less intact, have been desecrated and turned to base uses. Toul (Meurthe-et-Moselle) has to-day for its parochial churches its former cathedral and the collegiate church of St.-Gengoult, while its parish churches proper have disappeared, and constantly one comes across instances of desecrated churches. At Rouen St.-Laurent serves for a museum. At Caen St.-Nicholas is a military store, St.-Étienne-le-Vieux a builder's warehouse, and St.-Gilles stands idle and unoccupied. At Senlis St.-Pierre is the town market and St.-Frambourg a coach-house. Even small towns like Beaugency (Loiret) and Tournus (Saône-et-Loire) have their desecrated churches of St.-Étienne and St.-Valérien respectively. There is something very pathetic about these sanctuaries that have been diverted from their sacred use, yet we would not be without them and are thankful that they have been preserved for our study, for their owners, or those responsible for them, are, as a rule, very courteous in allowing visitors to inspect them.

11. How Churches should be Seen

There is one very important guiding principle which is perhaps too often ignored by visitors to ancient

[1] The present general rule in France is to have one cathedral church for each Department. As in former times the episcopal sees were much more numerous, this arrangement has involved loss of cathedral status for a good many famous churches, such as Auxerre, Lisieux and Toul.

churches and that is the rule that every work of man should be viewed, considered and studied, if we would appreciate it aright, in the light of the purpose for which it was designed and made. Otherwise we must fail to come at an understanding of it. Ancient churches must therefore be studied as the outcome of man's Godward aspiration, as structures reared for His glory and for His worship, and built in a spirit of devotion and sacrifice acceptable to God in union with the one perfect Sacrifice pleaded at the altars within their walls. As Hooker wrote, " churches receive, as everything else, their chief perfection from the end which they serve." Accordingly to come upon a cathedral at the hour of Mass, or to surprise it at its intimate devotions at Benediction, is to see it at its best ; as something more than a *monument historique* existing by the care of the State and for the curiosity of the tourist. It helps to understand, better than when you visit it guide-book in hand, why its builders made it beautiful, why its history is one of all the hopes and aspirations, the joys and sorrows, the tears and laughter of the place.

CHAPTER II

ROMANESQUE—ITS ORIGINS

1. The Lack of Unity in the Middle Ages in the Country we know as France

In studying the architecture of France it has to be remembered that in the Middle Ages during the growth of European civilisation after the incursions of the Barbarians into the Roman Empire and all through the formative period of Gothic style there was no " France " in the sense in which we know it to-day. National unity was a slow growth and was only attained in France at a much later date than in England. The " France " proper of the Middle Ages was the old territory of the *Ile de France* and the adjacent district whose centre was in Paris. The Northern Provinces of Artois and Picardy and the greater part of the west—Normandy, Brittany, Maine, Anjou, Poitou, Guienne and Gascony—acknowledged in varying extent the sovereignty of Norman and Plantagenet kings of England for about four hundred years, from the eleventh to the fifteenth century. Burgundy, Auvergne, Savoy and Provence were under the authority of their respective dukes or counts and only gradually came under the rule of the kings of " France " whose capital was Paris. Nor are the territories of these provinces or the spheres of influence of their rulers capable of very clear definition at given periods. At times portions of the north-east acknowledged the suzerainty of the Empire and the rulers of Burgundy held sway over a very large territory, having the seat of their government now at Geneva, now at Dijon and at another time as far south as Lyon. These old provinces, having for centuries their own independent or quasi-independent life and being at times hostile to one another, it is natural that we should find the great movements of western architecture receiving a peculiar impress and the style of building undergoing certain characteristic modifications according to the variations of the resources, materials and racial genius of the peoples of the several provinces. At the close of the Mediæval period the tendency towards centralisation and unity was hindered by the wars of religion. The Huguenots under Coligny and Condé and later La Rochelle in its resistance to Richelieu were contending against the spirit and need of the age. It was Richelieu's greatness as a statesman that he saw this and in the light of his vision so directed events as to bring unity, and the strength that flows therefrom, to his distracted country. But by the seventeenth century the great Gothic development in architecture had worked itself out and had given way before the revived taste for classical style, the effect of which was to obliterate, to a great extent, national or local expression in the art of building.

2. The Common Influence in Mediæval France

Throughout the provinces of old France there was, however, a common influence at work. From one source the stream of architectural style originally sprang, though receiving local colour in a country so large and populated in different parts by men of varying genius and racial qualities. It was said that all roads led to Rome. Certainly it was from Rome, along the lines of advance of her stupendous empire that all the architectural styles of the western world since her day diverge. Roman influence travelled through Gaul by two chief routes, and the buildings that have grown up along her lines of traffic while bearing the unmistakable Roman impress exhibit, accordingly, the traces of two rather different strains. First there is the Græco-Roman influence evident in Provence and northwards up the valley of the Rhône. Then, clearly distinguishable, we find a Romano-Byzantine strain following great lines of Roman enterprise and traffic to Ravenna and Venice, thence westwards to Narbonne and so northwards to Périgord, Poitou, Saintonge and the central provinces of France.

3. Roman and Romanesque in Provence and the Rhône District

The Romans who travelled to Trans-Alpine Gaul by the great road of the Via Aurelia would meet at Massilia (Marseilles) or at Aquæ Sextiæ (Aix-en-Provence) with a people of Greek ancestry, descendants of immigrants from Ionia, who, as early as the seventh century B.C. had founded a colony at Massilia and extended themselves thence. Massilia had prospered and established further colonies along the Mediterranean coast, eventually becoming in turn the ally and the subject of Rome. Life in that part of the empire was accordingly Roman, but touched with Greek thought, sentiment and taste. Up the Rhone valley and then on—northward through Burgundy and westward into Auvergne—flowed the stream of Græco-Roman influence. In this part of France life was as civilised and as Roman as in Italy, or as in Rome itself. This is evident from the historic monuments that remain to this day. These are so fine, so numerous and so well-preserved that it is here, in the old province of Trans-Alpine Gaul, that we are better able than elsewhere to reconstruct for ourselves the life of ancient Rome. Nor can we suppose that the buildings remaining, and exhibiting the style of imperial Rome unchanged, stood alone ; they must be survivals from a much greater number that once covered the land. Every part of the South of France possessed fine specimens of buildings raised for all the various purposes of life by the Roman conquerors. There were triumphal arches like those that delight us at Orange (Vaucluse) and St.-Rémi (Bouches-du-Rhône). Temples were reared in the Corinthian style which the Roman had made his own and of which he has left us examples in the Maison Carrée at Nîmes and the Temple of Augustus and Livia at Vienne (Isère). There must have been many a dainty little structure or monument like the "mausoleum" at St.-Rémi, and the mighty Pont-du-Gard planned as an aqueduct for bringing a fresh water supply to the city of Nîmes still spans the chasm of the Gardon with its triple tier of arches. Then of theatres we have on a grand scale those of Arles, Orange and—best preserved of all—Nîmes, while Vaison-la-Romaine gives us an idea, such as we can gain nowhere else perhaps save at Pompeii, of the ordinary life and structures of a Roman town. To one who may not have seen Roman remains outside a museum, or who has merely looked dully at a few foundations which he was told were Roman walls, the old cities of Provence are a revelation bringing the reality of Rome's greatness before his eyes with such vividness that he almost forgets the remoteness of Roman life and civilisation.

But over these fair provinces swept the tide of Barbarian invasion, and for a time it seemed as though the civilisation of the west must go down before their onset. Many of the Roman buildings disappeared, either through the devastation committed by the advancing hordes, or through their demolition by the inhabitants who seized upon their material in order to erect more effective defences against attack. But many things after all were not greatly changed by the dissolution of the Empire. The mingling of the old Roman spirit with the blood, the taste and the art of Asiatic Greeks, remained and lived on under the Goth, and under the guidance of Christianity. The influence of imperial Rome was too mighty a matter to be swept away by Barbarians, Burgundians or Saracens in those centuries when southern Gaul lay waste under their incursions from north and south. The early Christian builders were so imbued with the inherited classical ideal and so accustomed to its visible embodiment and presence in the magnificent monuments around them that it was a living force to the builders of the early Middle Ages. Accordingly we are able to trace the rise of a Christian Architecture, modelled upon the Roman, which became general by the tenth century wherever Roman rule had been. The Roman works themselves became the original models which the earlier buildings of the South of France closely followed, and they determined in many ways the character of the later architecture of the land.

As Roman influence was permanent, so, too, southern France and the Rhône district kept its contact with the Greek life of the eastern Mediterranean. The dedication of the church of St.-Trophime at Arles bears its testimony to the bringing of Christianity to the Delta of the Rhône by missionaries from Ephesus [1] and intercourse with the Greek East was in early Christian times continually renewed. To their brethren in Asia and Phrygia the churches of Vienne and Lyon sent an account, still

[1] The St.-Trophime to whom the church at Arles is dedicated is Trophimus the Ephesian mentioned in Acts xx. 4, xxi. 29, as a companion of the Apostle St. Paul.

extant, of their trials and persecutions. In view of this intercourse it is not surprising that in some of the details of the early Romanesque architecture the influence of Greek taste appears and the Greco-Roman detail of the Roman structures of Provence reappears in the Christian churches, so that we meet with fluted pillars in the wonderfully elaborate façades of St.-Trophime at Arles and of St.-Gilles (Gard). In the sculpture of the portals of these same two churches we find the acanthus leaf, the "Doric fret" and the Ionic "egg-and-dart" moulding, while Corinthian capitals occur in these examples and in the cathedral of Valence.

But while the details, such as capitals and mouldings, show the influence of the Greek East, the general lines of the buildings follow the Roman pattern, so that the term Romanesque is justified as a name for the style of architecture that emerged by the tenth century under Christian influence after the model of Roman structures. The main features of the plan of the Romanesque churches of southern France may be stated shortly as follows:

The building is cruciform with nave and aisles after the model of the Basilica, and the intersection of nave, transepts and chancel is covered by a central tower usually octagonal, a feature of Byzantine origin, derived from the central dome of the early Greek cross plan. Thus, in fact, the western vaulted Romanesque church, with its central tower—the features of which were continued, with further development, in the succeeding Pointed styles—was in its origin a translation of the eastern cupola type into the terms of the western basilican church. Very commonly a tower was added also at the west end, as at St.-Martin d'Ainay at Lyon, Cruas (Ardèche) and in the typical churches of Auvergne.

The vaulting is of the "tunnel" or "barrel" form, a

mode of roofing evidently derived from Roman buildings of the kind of which we have a singularly interesting example in the "Temple of Diana" at Nîmes. Like the Romanesque churches of which it is a prototype, this building has three avenues—divided, however, by solid walls with niches—each covered by a barrel-vault and the centre avenue wider than those on either side of it, like the nave and aisles of a church. The vaults of the Romanesque churches are generally semi-cylindrical or barrel-vaults properly so called, as at St.-Martin d'Ainay Lyon, Valence Cathedral, the churches of Auvergne, St.-Sernin Toulouse, Lescar (Basses-Pyrénées), St.-Gaudens (Hte.-Garonne), and further north at St.-Étienne Nevers and St.-Benoît-sur-Loire (Loiret). But the simple vaults of these Romanesque churches often take a pointed form, the pointed arch being not uncommonly used in construction, both for vaulting and pier-arches, without any thought of transition to a Pointed style and without affecting the fenestration or other details of the building in any way. Thus the pointed barrel-vault occurs in Romanesque churches at Aix-en-Provence, St.-Trophime and St.-Honorat Arles, Orange, Autun and La Charité-sur-Loire (Nièvre) and in the west at Çivray (Vienne) and many other churches.

After the example of the Roman basilica, the Romanesque churches are terminated by an apse at the east end. In the case of smaller and simpler churches there is a single apse for the chancel, as at Avensan, Bégadan,[1] Bouliac, Pujols and St. André-de-Cubzac (Gironde), Rioux and Rétaux (Charente-Inférieure), Nourray (Loir-et-Cher) and Les-Aix-d'Angillon (Cher). In some examples we find three apses towards the east, one terminating the chancel and one at the end of each

[1] Avensan and Bégadan have polygonal apses, the others referred to are semi-circular on the plan.

aisle, as at Unac and the chapel of Notre-Dame-de-Sabart Tarascon-sur-Ariège (Ariège), La-Garde-Adhémar (Drôme), Caromb (Vaucluse), Mouthiers-sur-Boëme (Charente) and Veauce (Allier). In the case of cruciform churches, those that are more simply planned have very commonly three apses, one terminating the chancel and one projecting from the eastern side of each transept, as at St.-Lizier-de-Couserans (Ariège), Cruas (Ardèche), Chabrillan (Drôme), Courpière and Thuret (Puy-de-Dôme), St.-Maurice (Vienne),[1] Melle (Deux-Sèvres), Chemillé (Maine-et-Loire) and Sancergues (Cher). But it is in the greater churches that we are indebted to the French genius for the special development of the *chevet*[2] of the church, which was taken over into the Gothic development and became a permanent characteristic of the architecture of the land. To the choir was built an ambulatory or circumscribing aisle and from this aisle projected again a series of smaller apsidal chapels, which radiating from the aisle grouped around the great apse of the choir in the exterior view. We have noteworthy examples of such east ends in Romanesque churches at St.-Sernin Toulouse,[3] Brioude (Hte.-Loire), Notre-Dame-du-Port Clermont-Ferrand, Issoire, St.-Saturnin, St.-Nectaire (Puy-de-Dôme), Vézelay (Yonne), Tournus (Saône-et-Loire), St.-Étienne Nevers, St.-Benoît-sur-Loire (Loiret), Fontgombault (Indre), St.-Menoux and

[1] The remarkable church at St.-Maurice is Romanesque throughout. Its east apse is polygonal, as are also the transept ends to north and south, while from the eastern side of each transept projects a chapel with semicircular apse.

[2] *Chevet*, meaning "head," is the term properly applied by French writers to the east end of a church of whatever plan it may be, apsidal or rectangular. In popular usage it is very often specially restricted to the characteristically French arrangement of an apse with ambulatory and radiating chapels.

[3] At St.-Sernin five chapels radiate from the aisle of the choir, and two apses also project from the east side of each transept.

Châtel-Montagne (Allier), Le Dorat (Hte.-Vienne), Notre-Dame-du-Pré Le Mans and the abbey church of Fontevrault (Maine-et-Loire). Much less frequently the eastern chapels with their apses radiate directly from the apse of a choir which has no circumscribing aisle. Examples of this type of plan for the east end of a church occur at Agen Cathedral, Grand-Brassac[1] (Dordogne), Solignac[2] (Hte.-Vienne), Vigeois (Corrèze) and Bénévent-l'Abbaye (Creuse).

The buildings under review must not be thought of as in any way rude or barbarous; in the refinement of their sculptural ornament they are far in advance of the Romanesque of England, whether pre-Conquest or Norman, and their dominant characteristic is a monumental durability. There is nothing in architecture so suggestive of extreme age yet of a radiant and hale durability as the thick-set Romanesque churches of France south of the Loire, with their firm and prudent vaulting, their well-set central towers and the close grouping of their apsidal chapels. The Renaissance brought classic style into such relationship with modern life that this tenth and eleventh century Romanesque seems remoter than Greece or Rome: yet its buildings have none of that perilous frailty that belongs to the later Gothic and the idea of romance and ruin is associated with the pointed arch rather than the round. In the south, too, the Romanesque appeals more strongly to the imagination than the Gothic, because it is indigenous, more sympathetic and more in keeping with the country, whereas the Gothic is an importation which never seems quite at home.

[1] At Grand-Brassac the main apse is semi-circular, while the apsidal chapels projecting from it are polygonal.

[2] In this case the main apse and the easternmost chapel are polygonal.

4. The Romanesque of the South-West to the Loire

The other chief avenue by which Roman influence penetrated into Gaul was through the seaport of Narbonne and by the trade routes extending northwards from thence to Cahors, Périgueux, Angoulême, Limoges and Poitiers. The civilisation which extended along these lines was Roman with a strong Byzantine strain, which reached Narbonne by sea by way of Ravenna and Venice. This Romano-Byzantine civilisation of the south-west exercised its influence over the first movements of Christian art after the evangelisation of the country and made itself felt for centuries afterwards. It is recorded, for instance, that in Angoulême Greek priests resided for a long period in the eleventh and twelfth centuries. In Limoges was a street named the Street of the Venetians, and the enamel work for which that city became famous all over Europe was brought thither in the twelfth century, it is said, by Greeks from Byzantium.

From the Loire to Guienne the missionaries and organisers of the Christian Church were, in the third century, St. Martial, first bishop of Limoges, and St. Eutrope, first bishop of Saintes. Then followed in the fourth century the still more widely famous St. Hilary of Poitiers and St. Martin of Tours. In St. Hilary's own city there still stands, small but comparatively perfect, a building which may be rightly accounted the most ancient Christian edifice in France, the baptistery belonging to St. Hilary's Cathedral of the fourth century, though this date only applies to the lower story, the upper part having been added some three centuries later. Its dedication, like that of such baptisteries in general, is to St. John Baptist.[1] The ground has been raised around it, so that the apses at its north and south ends seem to stand in pits. The upper part is curious, with gables like Roman pediments and a surface decoration of blank arcading with triangular-headed or straight-sided arches. There is a good deal of similar work at the church of St.-Généroux (Vienne), which may, therefore, be of about the same age going back as far as the seventh century.

As an outcome of the work of St. Hilary and St. Martin were founded the Abbeys of St.-Jouin-de-Marnes and Ligugé, reckoned as the two most ancient religious houses of France. There followed the scarcely less famous Abbeys of St.-Florent-le-Vieil on the Loire (end of the fourth century), St.-Maixent (Deux-Sèvres) in

[1] In the early days of the Christian era the administration of Baptism was restricted to the chief church of a diocese, the Bishop himself being properly the minister of the Sacrament. After freedom of worship was granted under Constantine the Great, baptisteries were erected near each cathedral church, but detached from it. This was the general custom in the East. In the West also the baptistery was in early times a structure separate from the church, and often continued so until the eighth or ninth century. On the Continent a good many of these detached baptisteries remain near cathedral churches, and though at a later period many have been converted into churches and have undergone some alteration accordingly, their dedication in the name of St. John Baptist usually survives as a testimony to their original purpose and use. Besides the example of St.-Jean at Poitiers, baptisteries are still found in France at Le Puy, Aix-en-Provence, Fréjus (Var), Riez (Basses-Alpes) and Vénasque (Vaucluse) of dates varying from the fourth to the ninth century. In Germany bishops' churches also had their separate baptisteries, which have been turned as a rule at a later period into churches. An original baptistery, now known as St. John's Church, still exists near the cathedral in the cities of Augsburg, Maestricht, Mainz, Ratisbon, Spires and Worms. Italy was more conservative in this respect than other countries of western Europe. Out of Italy very few baptisteries as structures apart from the church were built after the ninth century, but in that country the custom of having a separate building near the cathedral for a baptistery continued to the fourteenth century, and the examples at Pisa, Florence, Lucca and Parma are well known.

the fifth century, Luçon in the sixth and Noirmoutier founded by St. Philibert at the close of the seventh century. From the same period dates the Abbey of St.-Michel-en-l'Herm and a little later amongst many monasteries those of St.-Jean-d'Angély (ninth century), Maillezais (tenth century) and Nieul-sur-l'Autise were of special note. During the troubled centuries of the successive incursions of invaders from north and south it was in the monasteries that literature and art found

Temple St.-Jean Poitiers (Ancient Baptistery).

refuge and were preserved, and from them emerged the distinctive Romanesque of a large district embracing the provinces of Poitou, Saintonge, Angoumois and Périgord. To this style the church builders of the region remained faithful after the evolution of the Gothic of the north. Between the Loire and the Gironde the old Romanesque churches were not rebuilt, nor, save in very few cases, did they receive Gothic additions, and their type, well-adapted to the local genius that was penetrated by Romano-Byzantine traditions, persisted long after the great Gothic cathedrals of the North had been reared.

From the main features of these churches of the south-west the work of two distinct schools may be discriminated :

(1) The work of the architecture of Poitou is chiefly distinguished by the elaborate adornment of the west façades and occasionally also of the transept ends of the churches. These recall the triumphal arches of ancient Rome by the intricate richness of their decoration. The typical Poitevin west façade comprises three stages. The lowest contains the main entrance to the church. In the smaller structures this is a single doorway with semi-circular head of many receding orders, all, as well as the capitals of the flanking shafts, most profusely adorned with intricate sculpture. This central doorway is commonly flanked by blank arches of narrower proportions in just the same manner as some Norman doorways in England are, such as the west doorways of Rochester Cathedral, of Iffley (Oxon) and of Portchester (Hants). The greater churches have three portals in the façade[1]. The stage above is usually covered with a surface arcading of the same character as the doorway below, and in the centre arch of the arcade is the window. Above is the gable, sometimes containing another window. The buttresses take the form of thick clusters of columns,[2] and those at the angles, in the more important churches, are crowned by turrets as at Notre-Dame-la-Grande Poitiers and St.-Jouin-de-Marnes (Deux-Sèvres). These subsidiary turrets, as well as the greater towers of the churches, are very commonly capped by blunt stone spires of the pine-cone pattern characteristic of the district.[3] The treatment usual upon the west façade is sometimes also given to a transept end, as in

[1] See below, pp. 78, 79. [2] See below, p. 68. [3] See below, p. 84.

MORIENVAL (OISE).
NORTHERN ROMANESQUE.

PÉRIGUEUX CATHEDRAL.
ROMANESQUE OF PÉRIGORD.

facing p. 32.

the very fine example of the north transept at Vouvant (Vendée), where above a splendid doorway of the local type is some elaborate figure sculpture in two tiers, the lower being a representation of the Last Supper, with above, the Ascension, the design occupying the whole transept front up to the gable, where, surrounded by angels, the ascending Christ stands in the attitude of benediction. More rarely the profuse surface decoration commonly employed upon the west façade appears also upon the walls of the apse. These in the dainty examples at Rioux and Rétaux (Charente Inférieure) have richly adorned blank arcading and the walls are covered with panels of incised scaly pattern, trellis-work or other surface ornament. Within, the effect of these churches is solemn and grand. There is neither triforium nor clerestory ; the nave is covered with a barrel-vault after the Roman pattern and the aisles, as a rule, by a half-barrel or vault of quadrant form leaning against the nave.

(2) The second school of Romanesque of the south-west may be called the Périgordine, because the building which represents it most fully and completely is the remarkable Cathedral of St.-Front at Périgueux. The essential feature of the structures of the school is the method of vaulting with domes upon pendentives. Just as the barrel-vault is derived from a Roman pattern, so the domical vaults of Périgord are an indication of Byzantine origin and go back to the Eastern conception of a structure with a centralised plan, as opposed to the Latin and Western conception of a long hall after the basilican pattern. At St.-Michel-sur-Charente (Charente) we have an example of completely centralised plan, the church there being an octagon with eight radiating apses. But usually the Périgord builders followed a compromise between the Byzantine and Basilica conceptions and roofed a long nave with a series of shallow domes over

the bays. The churches of the type are extremely simple in design, having neither aisles nor triforium. The story of a Venetian colony at Périgueux is scarcely required to prove that the example of San Marco was followed there. The same words would describe the plan and main design of both churches. The plan is a Greek cross covered by five domes, one over the centre, one over the nave, one over the choir and one over each transept. Each of the domes stands upon four broad arches, and the four piers upon which the central dome stands consist each one of a square group of smaller piers connected into one by narrow arches. Then at the east end there is an apse. The still earlier church of St.-Étienne-de-la-Cité in the same city shows, in the two bays that remain of it, the same planning. The main arches supporting the domes are pointed, but without any hint of a transition to the Pointed style, which came in the North at least a century later. In these southern lands the pointed arch was specially used in certain parts of a building for structural reasons, but never seems to have been employed for the sake of beauty. We come across it mingled with the semi-circular form belonging properly to the Romanesque in the Cathedral of Cahors, in the ornamental arcading of the façade at Notre-Dame-la-Grande Poitiers and of the apse at Rétaux (Charente-Inférieure). Very occasionally the pointed form is used for doorways that have characteristic Romanesque adornment and round-headed windows above, as at St.-Martin d'Ainay Lyon and Blasimont (Gironde), but there is no evidence anywhere of a tendency to produce a pointed style, and doorways or windows are almost always round-headed. Next to the churches of Périgueux must be mentioned the Cathedral of Cahors with its two great domed bays for a nave, to which a choir has been added not of the original design and belonging to the Mid-Gothic period. The domes of this church are the largest of their style and give to the interior an air of noble simplicity and space, while the broad arches that bear them have an expression of immense power. It is the greatest of the early examples of a type of domed church developed in this part of France which have neither transepts nor aisles. The plan is the simplest possible, consisting merely of two or three squares in line, each one roofed by a dome. We have examples at Plassac, Brassac, Roullet and Fléac (Charente). In other instances the transepts are retained, as at Souillac (Lot) and in the Cathedral of Angoulême. There are in these cases also apsidal chapels opening out of the transept eastwards and others radiating from the apse at the east end. The interior at Angoulême is stately and impressive, if a little dull and cold, but its western façade is covered with sculpture, recalling that of Notre-Dame-la-Grande at Poitiers. Amongst the figure-sculpture of the twelfth century in this part of France we cannot help noting the fondness for representing figures on horseback on a large scale. Thus at Angoulême we have depicted St. George slaying the dragon and St. Martin sharing his cloak with the beggar, and similar equestrian figures appear on the elaborate façades at St.-Hilaire Melle and Notre-Dame Parthenay-le-Vieux (Deux-Sèvres), Surgères (Charente-Inférieure), Château-neuf-sur-Charente (Charente), Ste.-Croix Bordeaux and Çivray (Vienne). Amongst domed churches on a large scale must be classed St.-Hilaire at Poitiers, a very imposing church with double aisles, the inner ones extremely narrow and the outer ones of more usual span. Its most curious feature is the intricate system of pillars and arches of the vault consequent upon this arrangement.

Of the churches of Angoumois and Saintonge in general

it may be said that they combine the dominant features of the two schools whose work we have been considering—the domical vaulting of the style of Périgord with the ornate Poitevin façade, as the Cathedral of Angoulême does. All the valley of the Charente with the district about it abounds with village churches of this very attractive type of Romanesque in which east and west meet and are friends. A mere list of these would be tedious, but special reference may be made to the churches at Roullet, Plassac, Fléac, Chatres, Gensac, St.-Léger Cognac (Charente), Médis, St.-Romain-de-Benet, Sablonceaux, Talmont, the crypt of St.-Eutrope Saintes and the Abbey church of Notre-Dame (now enclosed in the *caserne* and desecrated) in the same city, Pont-l'Abbé-d'Arnoult, Corme-Royal and Écurat (all in Charente-Inférieure).[1]

Perhaps this is the most appropriate place to note a curious class of structure, the greater number of examples of which occur in this part of France, known as the *Lanterne des Morts*. These are slender towers, generally in a burial-ground, but not always so placed, with a receptacle near the top to carry a light. They vary in date from the eleventh to the thirteenth century, and are memorials of the days when instead of tolling the church bells lights gleamed through the openings of these curious towers, and the people of the town or of the countryside knew that one of their number had been called home to God.[2] The tower bearing these lanterns sometimes is designed as a cluster of Romanesque shafts, similar to those which serve as buttresses for the façades

[1] The magnificent portals of churches of this class are particularly dealt with below, p. 79.

[2] A similar idea has been adopted in some recent War Memorials as at Burwash in Sussex, where a lamp in the head of the Memorial is lighted upon the anniversary commemoration of those whose names are inscribed below.

of the churches, and the lantern is capped by a short spire of the pine-cone pattern common in the district. Both these features occur in the twelfth century examples at Cellefrouin (Charente) and Fénioux (Charente-Inférieure). These *Lanternes des Morts* are found in Deux-Sèvres, at Pamplie, a rude circular example; in Vienne, at Antigny (thirteenth century), Château Larcher (twelfth century), Journet (twelfth century), Moussac (twelfth century); in Charente, at Cellefrouin (twelfth century) and Pranzac (twelfth century); in Charente-Inférieure, at Fénioux (twelfth century) and St.-Pierre-d'Oléron (thirteenth century); examples also occur at Felletin (Creuse) of the thirteenth century, Culhat (Puy-de-Dôme) of the twelfth century, at Oradour-St.-Genest (Hte.-Vienne), Ciron and St. Genou (Indre) and farther north at Bayeux (Calvados) and at Orry-la-Ville (Oise). The last is a curious structure quite unlike the other examples referred to, being a plain and somewhat ungainly four-sided pyramid standing on open arches. Another *lanterne* of unusual form is the spire-like erection with Flamboyant tracery set within the church in the choir at Trèves (Maine-et-Loire).

CHAPTER III

ROMANESQUE—ITS FURTHER LOCAL VARIETIES

1. The Development of a Characteristic Style in Auvergne

As the Romanesque of the south moved up the valley of the Rhône and branched off into Auvergne it came into a country with a very marked character of its own and passed into the hands of a school of builders who gave the style almost as distinctive an architectural impulse as that which flowered a century or more later and on a vastly larger scale in the Gothic of the Ile de France. Auvergne is one of the most picturesque provinces of France and its picturesque character is derived from its volcanic origin. It is a land where every height bears signs of having once sent forth its pillars of cloud and smoke. Its towns mostly stand on the crest or the slope of some volcanic eminence springing from the plain and are darkly individual with narrow streets and tall black houses. Almost all are distinguished by one of those ancient swarthy churches with great central mass, axial towers, western narthex and curious incrustations of polychrome lava which are the marks of the local treatment of the Romanesque style.

The whole aspect of the Auvergnat churches is of the south. The local builders loved columns and half-columns, they used the barrel-vault and employed no pointed arches. About their work there is dark solidity and a general absence of ornament except upon the capitals of the columns and in the bands and panels of inlaid work, which are a special feature of Auvergne and will be noted presently. The plan is cruciform with central tower. This tower is generally an octagon, but it does not rise, as elsewhere, merely from the roofs of the nave and transepts. It stands upon a broad mass rising above the rest of the church, which forms a noble base for it and is alike externally and internally the most distinguishing feature of the Auvergnat type of church. In this remarkable arrangement the central part of the transept, for a space corresponding to the breadth of the nave and aisles, is raised a story above the nave roof. The central division of this raised part supports the octagonal lantern tower, while the lateral divisions have roofs that slope to north and south, and below the eaves of these roofs are windows above the transept roofs. The whole forms an admirable and dignified design for a central feature, and appears in the chief churches of the district at Notre-Dame-du-Port Clermont-Ferrand, Issoire, Orçival, Riom, St.-Nectaire, St.-Saturnin (Puy-de (Dôme), Brioude (Hte.-Loire), as well as at Chauriat where the central tower is square. The churches of Donzère and La-Garde-Adhémar (Drôme) are of kindred design in having their towers in the former case a square, in the latter an octagon, raised upon a central mass, and there is an example farther north in the church of the Madeleine at Tournus (Saône-et-Loire), which though different in its details recalls the Auvergnat arrangement. Thuret (Puy-de-Dôme) exhibits the local arrangement so far as the transepts and central feature are concerned, but the effect of it is neutralised by a lofty clerestory added to the nave. Seen from the inside the Auvergnat arrangement of the crossing increases the effect of height and further supplies an additional pair of lofty arches to increase the complication of arches crossing one another, some measure of which is necessarily found in any cruciform church. The interiors of the churches abound with groupings of small shafts and arches which are a marked feature of

ST.-NECTAIRE (PUY-DE-DÔME).

the style. The peculiar planning brings in a good many blank spaces and each space of the kind is used to make an unglazed window within the church. Such openings are especially common over the lantern arches.

In the grander examples there is a square tower at the west end in addition to the central octagon. We have this arrangement at Notre-Dame-du-Port Clermont-

Ferrand, at Issoire and at Brioude. St.-Nectaire and Mauriac (Cantal) have the unusual disposition for Auvergnat Romanesque of two towers at the west end in addition to the central feature : Riom, St.-Saturnin and Orçival are without their western towers. The western towers, like the central octagons, spring from a special base of their own ; this is a sort of western transept the lower stage of which forms a narthex, opening by one or more arches into the church. Another stage above also opens into the church by wide arches or in some cases by coupled shafted openings like unglazed windows. Externally the western fronts and towers are almost devoid of ornament, and they have such lack of shape about them as to be ungainly.

Viewed from without, these churches do not appear to have aisles. The church has lofty side walls which are thus treated with arcades and windows in two stages. In the lower range the windows are placed under bold and wide blank arches and these windows light the aisles. Above these an arcade of small arches and shafts has some of its members pierced as windows : these serve to light a gallery above the aisles. Within, above the lofty piers and below the spring of the barrel-vault, there runs an open arcade fronting the same gallery over the aisles. Thus within, this passage-way over the aisle vault appears as a triforium, while without it is treated as a clerestory whose lights are in the same wall as the aisle windows below.

In the churches of Auvergne there is the usual clustering of chapels around the great apse at the east, but with one or two local peculiarities. The easternmost chapel of all is square-ended sometimes as at Issoire, with the result that the mingling of curved and rectangular forms is scarcely pleasing to the eye. The straight-sided gables behind the sub-apses, as at Notre-Dame-du-Port Clermont-

Ferrand, Issoire and St.-Nectaire, also seem to introduce a confusion of lines. Still, the whole effect is certainly very good, and there is another local peculiarity which gives some added sweep and dignity to the piled-up mass of the chevet : this is the spacing out of the radiating chapels and the insertion of a window in the ambulatory of the choir between each chapel. This detail in the design of an east end is occasionally met with elsewhere, as at Fontgombault (Indre).

We have reserved till last a reference to the treatment of wall surfaces with inlaid pattern work of dark volcanic stone mingled with material of lighter colour, which is an adornment regularly employed in the churches of Auvergne and to which the nearest parallel elsewhere is afforded by the *flush-work* of East Anglia, whereby the exterior walls of so many Norfolk and Suffolk churches are ornamented with black-and-white patterns in flint and stone. In Auvergne the voussoirs of arched openings, doorways, windows, etc. are generally of alternate dark and light stone. At Brioude the central octagon is striped, while at Issoire and St.-Amable Riom the central towers have panels of diaper in checky and other patterns. The west tower of Notre-Dame-du-Port at Clermont-Ferrand is similarly panelled with chequered work, and there is an inlaid cross in the gable of the façade below. The south transept gable is also diapered all over with a large cross of stars within circles in the centre. Most characteristic of all is the deep band of inlaid work that runs round the great apse above the windows, generally in the form of stars within circles. This occurs at Brioude, Notre-Dame-du-Port Clermont-Ferrand, Issoire, St.-Nectaire and St.-Saturnin (Puy-de-Dôme). It is varied at Orçival by panels of lozengy pattern between the windows of the apse, and a deep band of lozenge-work also occurs in the chapel to the east of the transept at St.-Amable Riom. At Issoire panels in the sub-apses of the chevet have diapers of various patterns. At Brioude the lateral doorways of the west front have their tympana filled with flush-work of trellis pattern. It is however at Chauriat that work of the kind appears in the greatest profusion, the transept

CHAURIAT (PUY-DE-DÔME).

ends and side-walls of the nave being covered with inlaid diaper of checky, lozengy and starry patterns. Smaller churches in this part of France commonly exhibit this use of contrasted material in the voussoirs of arched openings, as at Langogne (Lozère), and in horizontal banding of towers with panels of chequered pattern, as at Perrier (Puy-de-Dôme). It is in the adjoining district of Velay, also a volcanic region, that this kind of natural polychrome is seen in a church of the largest scale in the cathedral of Le Puy. Besides the usual treatment of all arched openings with stones of alternate dark and light colour the whole imposing west façade is at Le Puy horizontally striped, and the blank arches in its upper part are filled with diapered patterns. The whole of the transept gables are filled in with various patterns and in the beautiful little cloister the wall-space above the arcade is finely diapered. In the same city of Le Puy the graceful little octagonal Romanesque building known as the Temple of Diana has a decoration in lozenges above the ornamental arcading of its walls, and the diminutive church of St.-Michel perched upon its tall needle of rock has its façade striped with diapered patterns in its blank arches.

Though Auvergne is the district where decoration by natural polychrome is most frequently employed in France and in the most original manner, there are other examples of its use, and this will be the most convenient place to notice them. Italy, having abundant available material in its coloured marbles, was the natural home of polychrome building. Sometimes this takes the form of panelling, as in Giotto's campanile at Florence and in the church of Santa Croce in the same city, where the groundwork is of light colour with panels outlined in darker marbles. More often the walls are built in horizontal courses of contrasting colours, as at Lucca, Cremona Cathedral, Sta.-Maria-Maggiore Bergamo, Siena, Orvieto and Genoa Cathedrals and San Zenone Verona. In France the Cathedrals of Digne (Basses-Alpes) and Embrun (Hautes-Alpes) are striped with horizontal courses in the Italian manner, and the same method of decorative building has been adopted for the modern cathedral of Marseilles. Tarbes Cathedral (Hautes-Pyrénées) also has in its apses horizontal courses, in this case of pink and cream-colour alternately, together with checky patterns.

In some churches of the Rhône valley there occurs a curious inlaid decoration of contrasted red and white material. Rude figures of animals of a Byzantine character are thus introduced in a frieze below the belfry windows of the west tower of St.-Martin-d'Ainay at Lyon, and beneath there is a large cross of circles and lozenges. Similar adornment is employed around the apse of the Cathedral at Lyon and occurs also at St.-Maurice Vienne (Isère).

It is not uncommon in any part of France to find the stones of arches of alternate dark and light colour, as at Vézelay (Yonne), and occasional examples are met with of the use of alternate materials in horizontal courses, as in the finely striped brown and white interior of the nave of Le Mans Cathedral, or the exteriors of the churches at Arques (Pas-de-Calais) and Vielles (Eure). Horizontal courses of brick and stone occur in the pillars at St.-Philibert-le-Grandlieu (Loire-Inférieure) and sometimes in the north as at Nesle-l'Hôpital (Somme). Normandy has a good deal of checky pattern in brick or flint and stone, occurring chiefly in châteaux and domestic buildings of which the Manoir Ango (Seine-Inférieure) is a splendid example, but a good instance of checky pattern in brick and stone is the chapel of the Château of St.-Germain-de-Livet (Calvados). At St.-Aubin Vieil-Évreux (Eure) the whole exterior of the church is covered with a chess-board pattern, and on a larger scale the churches of St.-Valéry-sur-Somme (Somme) and Le Tréport (Seine-Inférieure) have their walls adorned with a striking arrangement of waving checky-pattern.

The cathedral of Le Puy has just been referred to as a very remarkable example of natural polychrome decoration on a large scale, and this seems the place to notice it in fuller detail as it is situated in the volcanic district of central France, though in its style it is altogether distinct from the churches of Auvergne and indeed is a great church which stands alone, having no following and having set the example for no local type. Its unique feature is accounted for by its wonderful situation on the steep slope of a huge volcanic rock from the Rocher Corneille, at the summit of which the gilded image of Notre-Dame de France looks over a city which a famous artist designated the most beautiful in the world. The unique feature referred to is the planning of the west end, where the ground falls so abruptly that one approaches by flight upon flight of steps. The three tall entrances in the ground story of the façade open, not into the church, but into a kind of crypt, very massively built, which extends beneath the two westernmost of the six bays of the nave and from this large crypt-porch stairways lead up on either side to the level of the pavement of the church, which is at the same level as the external string-courses above the lateral arches of the ground story. Thus the nave has no west door, but only lateral entrances and is lighted at this end by the three windows of the middle stage of the front. As originally planned this great western entrance on a steep slope must have been even more impressive than it now is, for then the steps went up in a direct line reaching the level of the floor of the church beneath the central dome at the crossing. It looks as though the extraordinarily impressive conception of such an entrance to a church was gradually evolved. What was originally a flight of steps leading up to a west door, would as the nave grew westward by several bays be gradually swallowed up within the church, the floor of the church forming a roof that became longer and higher over the deepening portal. The east end has features nearly as interesting. A campanile stands almost touching the east end of the north aisle. It has the markedly receding stages that are to be observed in other towers of the southern Romanesque, such as those of St.-Trophime at Arles and the Cathedral of Angoulême. It shares also with the towers of a Limousin group of which characteristic examples occur at St.-Léonard (Hte.-Vienne), Collonges and Uzerche (Corrèze) and Brantôme (Dordogne), a peculiar detail of design by which the top octagonal story springs from behind sharply pointed and boldly projecting gables that rise above the large lights of the stage below. As regards its general aspect, it groups with the octagonal lead-covered dome of the crossing in a thoroughly Italian manner. The choir is of one bay only and is square-ended. Between this short choir and the south transept, upon an elevated platform is a very striking porch, with its east and south sides open beneath wide and boldly moulded arches. Then in front of these arch-mouldings there are free arches detached from the arch above and standing upon diapered pillars, while radiating from the free arch are three short columns like spokes connecting it with the arch above. There is no exact parallel to it and it is like an anticipation in Romanesque of the pierced fringes of tracery that adorn the doorways of the Gothic of the fifteenth century, or we may say that it bears a relation to them such as the flying buttresses of Chartres with their radiating short pillars bear to some of the lace-like buttresses of the Flamboyant style. The interior is alike curious and impressive. The bays of the nave are roofed with domes—though these do not show from the outside with the exception of the one at the crossing, being covered by a long roof. Each dome is carried upon transverse arches supporting a wall pierced by arched openings, the effect being to give to each bay a rectangu-

St.-Léonard (Haute-Vienne).

lar lantern, lighted by the clerestory, with a domical roof. Each bay, in fact, has an internal appearance exactly similar to that of a central tower. Elsewhere in the

ST.-SERNIN TOULOUSF.

SOUTHERN ROMANESQUE.

facing p. 48.

church the vaulting is varied: in the aisles it is quadripartite, while the short choir and its aisles have barrel-vaults, the choir being separated from its aisles by solid walls, as in England at Rochester Cathedral.

2. Burgundian Romanesque

As "Burgundy" is a somewhat vague term denoting a district of varying extent and having different political centres at different times, so while the current Romanesque was adopted it did not undergo such marked or distinct development such as we have been able to trace in the churches of Auvergne, Périgord, Saintonge and Poitou. The most notable influence, both religious and architectural, in this part of France in the eleventh century must have been that of the great Benedictine Abbey of Cluny, whose church was one of the longest ever built, measuring 580 feet in external length, and carried a group of eight towers. Unfortunately it has perished except the southern arm of the main transept; for it had a second transept farther to the east, a feature of ground-plan not followed elsewhere in France, though in England it was adopted at Canterbury, Rochester, Lincoln,[1] York, Salisbury and Worcester Cathedrals, and at Beverley Minster. Another outstanding feature of the plan at Cluny was a large narthex or ante-church at the west end, and this conception seems to have influenced the builders, at least of the greater churches, of this part of France. Tournus (Saône-et-Loire) has at its west end between two towers and with a roof ridge higher than the nave, a narthex of plain and early character. Paray-le-Monial (Saône-et-Loire) also has a narthex between

[1] St. Hugh of Lincoln was connected with Cluny and must have known its plan, and it was under him that the English minster received its second transept.

its western towers, but not reaching to the height of the nave. The grandest example of the kind is at the church of the Madeleine at Vézelay (Yonne). In this case also the narthex is between two west towers. It is entered by three splendid portals, the centre one a double one, adorned with the most elaborateRomanesque sculpture of the twelfth century, the church itself being entered from the narthex by a similar range of doorways still more beautifully ornamented. With this may be compared the western front of Autun, also with its pair of towers. The much smaller and more ancient church of St.-Pierre Vienne (Isère)—now desecrated and serving as a *Musée lapidaire*—also has an example of the closed porch or narthex. The deep arcaded porch at St.-Benoît-sur-Loire may perhaps be placed in the same class and is attributed to a date as early as the eleventh century. This imposing structure has no walls. It is wider than the nave, though not so wide as nave and aisles together, and stands boldly out from the west end of the church a great square of sixteen clustered piers supporting a quadripartite vault of nine square bays, the centre bay on the east side containing the entrance to the church; above is another story similarly designed and capped by a huge pyramidal roof. The conception of a grand deep porch for a western entrance persisted in this part of France and was continued in churches of the Gothic style. We find it in early Pointed at Beaune and Notre-Dame Dijon (Côte-d'Or) in the Mid-Gothic or "Decorated" in the lovely church of St.-Père-sous-Vézelay (Yonne) and in the later Gothic at Semur-en-Auxois and at Auxonne (Côte-d'Or). We see too a lingering of the same tradition in the strange colonnaded portico with oblong domical finish in the Renaissance church at Asfeld (Ardennes). It is to this fondness for a frontispiece to the church that we owe the cloister-like porches that sometimes extend across the façade of a church, as at Hermonville (Marne)—a fine Romanesque example in stone—Vieux-St.-Maur (Seine-et-Marne) and Baye (Marne), and constructed in wood at Sermaize (Marne), and Mulsans (Loir-et-Cher). Of these wooden cloister-porches the finest instance occurs at Bar-sur-Aube (Aube), extending not only across the west façade, but along the south side of the church.

The remaining fragment of the Abbey Church of Cluny shows us features which became usual in the Burgundian Romanesque. These are triforium and clerestory with barrel-vault above. The use of fluted pillars or pilasters is also characteristic of the Romanesque of this part of France. These occur in the pillars of the Roman temples at Nîmes and Vienne and in the Roman triumphal arches as at Orange and Autun. We have seen them in the portals of St.-Trophime Arles and of St.-Gilles and we meet them at Cluny, in Vienne (Isère) at the Cathedral of St.-Maurice and the church of St.-André, in the Cathedrals of Verdun and Autun, at Tournus (Saône-et-Loire), Langres Cathedral, at Paray-le-Monial (Saône-et-Loire), Romans (Drôme) and elsewhere.

The apses, except in the greater and more important churches, are often without aisles, as at St.-Paul-de-Varax (Ain), St.-Parize-le-Châtel (Nièvre), Druyes (Yonne) and Vignory (Haute-Marne) and the towers are frequently central, not only where there are groups of three as at Autun Cathedral, Tournus and Paray-le-Monial, but where the church has only one tower it is very commonly in the centre, as at Champs-le-Duc (Vosges), Druyes (Yonne), Til-Châtel (Côte-d'Or), Varax and Nantua (Ain), St.-Étienne Nevers, Rouy, St.-Parize-le-Châtel and Garchizy (Nièvre), St.-Sauveur (Loire) and St.-Paul at Lyon.

There are, further, churches of outstanding interest in this part of France which call for special mention. St.-Philibert at Tournus (Saône-et-Loire) has already been referred to in connection with its narthex, but much more remarkable is the method of vaulting adopted. It is carried on transverse arches as at the Cathedral of Le Puy, only instead of each compartment between these arches being roofed by a dome, these cross walls are, at Tournus, connected by a series of barrel-vaults lying transversely across the nave. The whole interior is impressive in its severity, for all is bald and bare, the great cylindrical pillars have only mouldings for capitals, reminding us of those at Gloucester Cathedral and Tewkesbury, while every arch is of a single order and quite plain. It is in the use of transverse barrel-vaults for its nave that the church is unique, such a method being rarely employed and if at all only on a small scale, as in the aisles of the church at Lescar (Basses-Pyrénées).

Nevers has the notable Romanesque church of St.-Étienne finished at the close of the eleventh century. It is a large cylindrical barrel-vaulted church, with a low octagonal lantern at the crossing, such as we meet with again at La-Charité-sur-Loire in this same neighbourhood, and there is a broad narthex-like mass of building at the west end such as is common in Germany, and characteristic of Burgundian churches. The crossing in the interior is treated in a curious and very effective manner. At about the triforium level an arch in line with the aisle walls of the nave and choir is thrown across each transept, then the wall extending from this arch to the barrel-vault of the transept is pierced by a series of five openings separated by four shafts. Thus a sort of triforium appears to be carried on large arches across the transept on either side. In this use of unglazed openings with shafts as a sort of internal wall decoration St.-Étienne Nevers resembles the churches of Auvergne.

At La-Charité-sur-Loire is a later church founded in 1133. The nave has been destroyed, but a large Gothic west doorway remains by the side of the majestic north-west tower adorned with elaborate surface-arcading. The site of the north aisle is occupied by a range of dwelling-houses, some of whose upper windows are set in the richly moulded arches of the triforium. The remaining portion of the nave has had its original character destroyed, but the choir and transepts are of the greatest interest and of solemn beauty. There are triforium, clerestory and pointed barrel-vault. Alike in the blank arcade of the triforium and in the arcading on the lower stage of the tower, the little arches are of cinquefoil form instead of plain semi-circular, following a fashion that is more common in the Romanesque of the Rhineland.

3. The Angevin Development of Romanesque

The Angevin is another of the varieties of style which sprang up in the eleventh and twelfth centuries to supplant the older Romanesque common to all western Europe. Its character is very marked and the name *Angevin* is not inappropriate for it, because Anjou is the headquarters of the prevalence of the type of building, though it extends to territory on either side. It was in the time of Henry II, King of England, who was also Count of Anjou, that this powerful and original development took place in his Continental domain, and in view of this some French writers have designated it as the *Plantagenet* style. In England during the reign of Henry II the transition from Norman to Early English was taking place. So too in Anjou we may say that the Angevin style was a local phase of Transition, but entirely different in its character from any contemporary movement elsewhere. Its general aspect is Romanesque. There is the same construction as in Romanesque elsewhere and also to a great extent there are the same details, but with all this we find a strong local preference for a certain type of plan and general effect, rather than strictly speaking, a difference of style. The Cathedral of Angers may be considered the greatest example of the Angevin type, and its plan is evidently derived from domed churches like Angoulême. Its ground plan shows three square bays for the nave, one for the crossing, one for each transept and one for the choir with a semi-circular apse beyond. There are no aisles, no pillars standing free and no architectural provision for any kind of chapel, the great sweep at the east end being the only apse. All aisles and piers being thus dispensed with, the builders of this school seem to have aimed at an effect of great breadth and space and to have used few and large members rather than many small ones. The proportions, indeed, are so wide and spacious that two bays of an Angevin church would make four of any other kind of design. An expression of great power is imparted by fine transverse pointed arches, carried by strong clustered shafts. This expression is still further enhanced by the treatment of the side walls, the lower part in each bay being occupied by a single great pointed arch stretching from base to base of the main piers, with above these a corbelled cornice and over that again tall round-headed windows, two in each bay. The Angevin vaulting is of the domical type derived like the planning from the churches of Périgord and Angoumois. In earlier examples of the style the vaulting takes the form of a simple dome built in horizontal courses over each bay as in the case of the crossing of the Abbey of Fontevrault (Maine-et-Loire) and at the church of

St.-Avit-Sénieur (Dordogne). But the typical Angevin vault has diagonal ribs, not that the vaulting is really quadripartite vaulting, but each bay is covered with a domical vault after the manner of Périgord, with groin-ribs as used in Anglo-Norman vaulting applied to it. The outstanding characteristics of churches of the type under discussion are, therefore, the wide aisleless avenue giving an impression of great breadth and space and the domical vaulting with added ribs. We find the Angevin vaulting in the Cathedrals of Angers and Poitiers and at St.-Serge and the Hospital in Angers. Vaults of this kind cover wide aisleless naves at the Cathedral and La-Trinité Angers, Ste.-Radegonde Poitiers, Notre-Dame-de-la-Coûture Le Mans, Laval Cathedral (Mayenne) and as far north as Pontorson (Manche). Other typical examples of Angevin style may be seen at Notre-Dame-d'Avénières Laval and at St.-Pierre and Notre-Dame-de-Nantilly Saumur. At the Cathedral of Le Mans, though the nave has aisles, distinct signs of Angevin influence may be marked in the work of William of Passavant in the twelfth century. He destroyed the former basilican design, making the arches pointed and turning each alternate column into a pier form which rises a vaulting shaft. Thus two pier-arches are under one bay of vaulting with its two clerestory windows, quite after the Angevin fashion.

It has been noted above that in the strictly Angevin plan there is no structural arrangement for side chapels, but in some cases there are shallow hollows in the walls within the church making small apses for altars, while the external wall is flat. This arrangement is seen in the nave of La-Trinité Angers, where beneath the wide arches upon the side walls there are apses hollowed out in each bay. The east end of the Cathedral of Poitiers shows a similar device. Externally it is formed by a broad flat wall covered by a wide-spreading roof that stretches over choir and aisles, but internally there is a range of three apses within the thickness of the walls. The same applies also to the transepts, each of which has on its eastern side an apse segmental on the plan, of which there is no indication externally.

Where a broad aisleless Angevin nave has been added to a choir of different architectural character, a curious and noteworthy internal feature results, the wide nave opening into the choir and transepts by a range of three arches, so that the vista terminates eastwards in a kind of triple chancel-arch. This peculiarity occurs at La-Trinité Angers where the central arch is narrow and has a still narrower one on either side of it, and there is a somewhat similar arrangement at Notre-Dame-de-la-Coûture Le Mans, where an Angevin nave has been added to a choir of earlier Romanesque character. Ste.-Radegonde Poitiers resembles the churches mentioned in that the view looking east from the nave is closed by the lofty central arch of the apse flanked by the tall and narrow arches of the ambulatory, giving an effect similar to that of the interior of Gerona Cathedral in Spain, the grandest example of an arrangement of the kind. Laval is another instance. In the cathedral there the chancel arch is very narrow and semi-circular, with on either side of it a pointed arch lower but of nearly the same span. The Abbey of Fontevrault and the church of St.-Ours at Loches may also be quoted as outlying churches sharing this peculiarity, though in these two last instances the side arches are so greatly reduced in width as almost to become mere hagioscopes. In the south at Orthez (Basses-Pyrénées) a wide aisleless nave of Angevin type opens into the chancel by three bold pointed arches, the centre one of greater height and breadth than those on either side.

The Cathedral of Poitiers departs from the Angevin plan in having aisles. It consists of three parallel avenues of equal length and nearly equal height, without triforium or clerestory, the interior forming a vast hall with its great vault upheld by fourteen clustered pillars in two rows of seven in each row. It thus forms a notable example of that type of design known as a *Hall-church.*[1] An early instance of the kind occurs in the Cathedral of Valence (Drôme) attributed to the eleventh century. The plan of Poitiers is that of Henry II's foundation dating from 1161 and it ranks amongst the grandest of the Hall-churches of Europe. The church of St.-Laurent at Le Puy shows a fully developed example in French Gothic, and there are other instances at St.-Michel-aux-Lions Limoges, Notre-Dame St.-Lo (Manche) and a late Gothic example at St.-Maurice Lille, with five parallel avenues, a nave and four aisles, separated by slender cylindrical columns, besides the Dominican churches of Toulouse.[2] In Germany the Hall-church became a characteristic development of ecclesiastical architecture and examples on a great scale are numerous, as the subjoined list shows :

Balne
Billerbeck (St. John).
Dantzig (Marienkirche).
Hameln (Minster).
Herford (Minster).
Herford (St. Mary-on-the-Hill).
Idensen.
Kirchlindt.
Kolberg.
Lemgo (St. Nicholas).
Lippstadt (Gr. Marienkirche).
Methler.
Münster (St. Ludger).
Paderborn.
Prenzlau (Marienkirche).
Soëst (Sta. Maria-in-Hohe).
Warburg (St. Nicholas).

[1] This is the technical name given to the plan arrived at by the juxtaposition of parallel avenues—generally three, but sometimes two as in the examples at Toulouse—instead of the usual arrangement of a nave with lateral aisles and clerestory.

[2] The Dominicans were a preaching Order, and their desire for an auditorium to accommodate a large congregation would influence them in the adoption of the plan in question.

To these should be added St.-Stephen's, Vienna.

The Hall-church is not common in England, but Bristol Cathedral is a fine example and in Devon and Cornwall the characteristic local type of church has two or three parallel avenues of about equal height and length gabled independently and without structural chancel. At Dantzig also the roofs are in parallel ridges, but in Germany generally the whole three avenues are brought within the span of one steep roof. In the French examples at Poitiers Cathedral and St.-Laurent Le Puy, there is also one wide roof covering nave and aisles, but its pitch is low.

Before leaving the region of domical vaults for a consideration of the more northern Romanesque, something must be said of the markedly individual church of St.-Ours at Loches (Indre-et-Loire). Some of its features have been already noted; its large western porch and its triple opening from the nave to the chancel, all three arches of semi-circular shape and the side ones so low and narrow as to have the appearance of open doorways. The plan is that of the Angevin churches, a nave of square aisleless bays—here two in number and set between a central and a western tower. Beyond the west tower is the porch and beyond the central tower a short chancel with apse. The aisles and chapels added later to the nave are not obtrusive in the internal effect. From short transepts with lean-to roofs small apsidal chapels project eastwards. But the singularity of Loches lies in the fact that the two bays of the nave are covered, not with domes but with octagonal spires of the type that is usual in the Romanesque churches of Touraine. A line of domes may be hidden beneath the ridge of a long roof, as in fact they are at the Cathedrals of Le Puy and Angoulême, but such treatment is scarcely possible with spires and the result is at Loches a serrated outline such as no other church possesses, the two spires which cover the nave bays standing in line with the two spires of the central and western towers. The interior view is equally remarkable, for the spire-vaults at Loches, like the domical vaults of Périgord, are open

LOCHES (INDRE-ET-LOIRE).

to the top, so that standing on the floor of the nave one looks up into these spires to their very apex.

4. THE ROMANESQUE OF NORMANDY AND THE NORTH

Here and there in France—in addition to the crypts of early Romanesque beneath some churches like the vast and notable ones at Chartres Cathedral and in the south at St.-Eutrope Saintes (Charente-Inférieure)—there still remain a few very early churches such as the Basse-Œuvre of Beauvais Cathedral, assigned to a date from the sixth to the eighth century. This, like the churches of Domagné (Ille-et-Vilaine) and Vieux-Pont-en-Auge (Calvados) exhibits in its walls the Roman manner of building with courses of flat bricks, such as we see in England in the massive walls of Richborough (Kent) or Burgh Castle (Suffolk). Other primitive buildings like the baptistery of St.-Jean at Poitiers and the church of St.-Généroux (Vienne) have semi-circular and straight sided forms of arch in their openings and surface arcadings. The herring-bone masonry characteristic of primitive building may also be seen in some early churches of Normandy, as at Parfouru-Léclin, Vienne and Ouilly-le-Vicomte (Calvados). The early sanctuaries, however, must have been for the most part sacrificed to the fury of the Northmen which became proverbial. It is noteworthy that buildings of the Romanesque era are relatively few and unimportant in northern France, and that it is in Normandy that they first began to arise on an imposing scale when the fierce Northmen had settled down and accepted the Christian faith.

Before the Norman Conquest of England the church builders of Normandy used the type of Romanesque generally current in the west in the tenth century; they adopted the basilica plan and the semi-circular apse and their structures were marked by a very sparing use of ornament. Few specimens of this earlier fashion of their building remain, but the Abbey of Jumièges (Seine-Inférieure), dating 1040–67, shows it on a large scale, and it appears rather akin to the Burgundian and German Romanesque, than to that development which we know as Norman and which followed the conquest of

England by Duke William.[1] In the remains of the Abbey of Bernay (Eure), founded by the Conqueror's grandmother Judith and unfinished at her death in 1024, we have another example of early Norman building. It is desecrated and used as a corn-store and its nave vaulting has been destroyed, but in its aisles it exhibits a domical vaulting akin to that of the Provinces south of the Loire. The Abbey Church of St.-Georges-de-Boscherville (Seine-Inférieure) was begun in 1050, but differs altogether from the earlier Abbey of Jumièges in character, and both by its general features and its profusely adorned doorways should be classed with post-Conquest Norman churches.

After the Conquest of England by Duke William there followed a period of extraordinary activity in building in the Norman dominions on both sides of the Channel. Of the church-building era that followed after the Normans had settled down from their incursions Raoul Gleber wrote in the middle of the eleventh century that "it was as if the world, shaking off its old tatters, desired to re-clothe itself in the white robes of the Church . . . all religious buildings, cathedrals, country churches, village chapels, were transformed by the faithful into something better." In England the Norman period was the great building era, affecting the whole country which had attained a national unity under the strong rule of the Norman kings. In France the great architectural expansion took place later and coincided with the development of Gothic Art. But the type of architecture we call Norman Romanesque was in vogue in the territory of the Norman kings alike in their homeland of Normandy and in their newly acquired

[1] Similarly the Pre-Conquest (Saxon) architecture in England has features connecting it with the Romanesque of the Rhineland. See *Parish Church Architecture*, pp. 88–90.

realm of England. For in the eleventh century and after a narrow sea was not much of a barrier. Roads scarcely existed, means of travel by land were bad and insecure and only available for the rich, whereas a sea made possible an intercourse that was scarcely possible over a serious distance by land. Normandy, in fact, was nearer to England than to Paris, and the Sussex coast, as its churches show,[1] had more in common with Normandy than with England that lay north of the Downs and the Weald. In architecture, as in other matters, during the prevalence of the Norman style and through the transition to early Pointed the blood of a common ancestry proved thicker than all the waters of *La Manche*.

In Caen, the Conqueror's own favourite city, the great building activity began. In pursuance of a penance laid upon them by the Pope for their marriage within the prohibited degrees William and his wife Matilda founded the two great Abbeys at Caen. It was under Lanfranc, afterwards Archbishop of Canterbury, that the work of building was carried on at St.-Étienne (the "Abbaye-aux-Hommes,") and the nave and west towers remain, the choir having been reconstructed later. The vault is sexpartite, probably the earliest extant of the kind and the triforium has wide open arches such as we see in England at Norwich Cathedral and at Southwell. The fellow foundation of La-Trinité, the "Abbaye aux Dames" was in building at the same

[1] There are chapels or clear traces of once existing chapels opening out from the east side of a transept in the Continental manner at Westham, Old Shoreham, New Shoreham, Sompting, Broadwater, Findon, and Burpham. At Burpham there is a remarkable undercut chevron ornament on an arch identical with one at Condé-sur-Laison (Calvados), and the pillars and arches of Transitional character at Burpham and Pagham resemble those of a church in Normandy rather than of an English church.

time and has retained its Norman choir and apse. The pier arches are loftier than at St.-Étienne, but the triforium has become a mere arcade, or series of round-headed panels upon the wall. Like that of St.-Étienne, the vault is round-arched, but it is not strictly sexpartite, it is a quadripartite vault with a transverse arch across the middle of each compartment supporting the crown of the vault. Both churches have the group of three towers that became characteristic of the Anglo-Norman plan for greater churches. Caen has another notable church of almost unaltered Romanesque in the church of St.-Nicholas, now desecrated, but in this case the present vaulting is of fifteenth-century date. With the Abbeys of Caen should be classed the Abbey of St.-Georges-de-Boscherville, begun just before the Conquest by Ralph de Tancarville, Chamberlain of the Conqueror. This is a fine cruciform Norman church with central tower and two of much smaller dimensions flanking the west front. The doorway in this front is one of the most elaborately adorned of the Romanesque portals of Normandy, and the arches at the entrance to the Chapter house are similarly enriched. Before we leave the greater churches of Normandy the Cathedral of Bayeux, the see of the Conqueror's half-brother Odo, claims attention. Here only the lower part of the nave is of Norman date. The arches of the main arcade have many mouldings, and the spandrels between them are covered with diapered patterns, interlaced lines, scales and other designs varied in each bay, the effect being similar to that of the "hatched" spandrels of the nave arcade at Christchurch (Hants). In the Department of Seine-Inférieure the nave and transepts of Graville-Ste.-Honorine and the nave of Étretat are fine examples of Norman Romanesque; the former has square piers with attached shafts with square-edged arches above.

Étretat has short cylindrical columns with a bold embattled ornament round its wide arches. Most of the village churches, especially in the Department of Calvados, exhibit familiar features of the Norman style and some are practically complete and unaltered examples. Ouistreham has a large church with central tower and finely arcaded west façade. Colombelles is another unaltered church of simpler character, also with central tower. Touques has a low central octagon. Often the tower is lateral, as at Biéville, Cintheaux and Huppain, and a great many of these Normandy churches have the rectangular chancel that we are familiar with in England, as Mouen, Cintheaux, Courcy, Beaumais, Touques, Ste.-Marie-aux-Anglais and Thaon. The shallow flat buttresses, emphatic corbel-tables and external arcading with abundant use of zigzag ornament are prevalent throughout, and many a little church with aisleless nave and rectangular chancel has an appearance like that of Barfreston (Kent), such as those of Mouen, Cintheaux and Haute-Allemagne. Thaon is further remarkable in having the blank arches of its exterior arcading filled in with a sort of diaper-work. We noted the use of an adornment of the kind in the interior of Bayeux Cathedral, and we meet with the same conception in the adornment of a wall surface in the trellis-pattern in strong relief which occupies the gables of the transept front at St.-Étienne Beauvais and of the west façade of the gem-like little Romanesque church at Trie-Château (Oise). In the Department of Oise, besides the nave and transepts of St.-Étienne Beauvais with the loftily proportioned and gracefully adorned transept façade, and the church of Trie-Château, Morienval with its uncommon grouping of three well-designed towers, one western and two flanking the apse, shows a Romanesque church on a large scale. The nave

ANGERS CATHEDRAL.

NOTRE-DAME-DE-LA-COÛTURE LE MANS.

ANGEVIN STYLE

facing p. 64.

of Évreux Cathedral is severe Norman, contrasting with its fifteenth-century Gothic choir. Manche has a fine Romanesque church with central tower in the Abbey of Lessay, and in the north, where Romanesque churches are much rarer, there is a fine instance of a complete church of the style at Lillers (Pas-de-Calais).

In the neighbourhood of Paris the notable church of Poissy (Seine-et-Oise) has good Romanesque work of the twelfth century, and in Paris itself are remnants only of a few churches of the style. St.-Martin-des-Champs has a vaulted choir and apse, the apse assigned to the eleventh century and the choir rebuilt in the twelfth. The old church of St.-Pierre on Montmartre, with its well-designed tower of deeply recessed and moulded lights, goes back to the twelfth century, and of the same date are Romanesque portions of St.-Julien-le-Pauvre and St.-Germain-des-Près.

CHAPTER IV

ROMANESQUE—ITS DETAILS

As has been pointed out above, the various local developments of architecture in the old Provinces of France were not exactly styles of architecture, but rather fashions of building in one general style, particular modes of using and adapting the common Romanesque of the West according to local genius or fondness for particular kinds of effect. In the preceding chapters an attempt has been made to distinguish the classes of Romanesque architecture in France. It now remains to treat of the details, whether of structure or ornament, that are more or less common to them all.

(A) Pillars and Arches

The main piers of the arcades are usually square with half-columns attached as in Auvergne at Notre-Dame-du-Port Clermont-Ferrand, Issoire and Brioude, or in the west at Notre-Dame-la-Grande Poitiers and Le Dorat (Haute-Vienne) or in the north as in the great abbeys at Caen. The vaulting shafts are also commonly carried up in front of such large piers. Sometimes we have clusters of tall pillars as at St.-Hilaire Poitiers. Less frequently the pillars of the nave arcade are cylindrical, as in the early examples at St.-Martin-d'Ainay Lyon and St.-Philibert Tournus; the former short and slight in proportion after the classical model,[1] the latter tall and massive. Cylindrical columns are also met with in churches of the Norman Romanesque, as at Étretat. Where there is an ambulatory to the choir the stilted narrow arches of the apse are borne on circular columns. The main arches of nave arcades are round, as also the heads of windows, so also generally the shape of barrel-vaults and doorways and ornamental arcades is semi-circular. But the pointed barrel-vault is not uncommon and in doorways and façades we sometimes have a mingling of round-headed and pointed arches, though without any sort of hint of a transition to another style of building. Such mingling of pointed and rounded arches is very noticeable at the Cathedral of Cahors, in the façades of St.-Martin d'Ainay and Notre-Dame-la-Grande Poitiers and in the apse at Rétaux (Charente-Inférieure). More rarely in the southern and Burgundian Romanesque we come across arches with trefoil heads in surface arcading or in small openings. The very fine tall central octagon at Le Dorat (Hte.-Vienne) has an arcading of this form and we find the same form in small arches at Issoire and the Cathedral of Le Puy. The little chapel of St.-Michel-d'Aiguilhe at Le Puy has a large trefoil arch above its main doorway, and the tower of St.-Pierre at Vienne (Isère) has it above the lights in one of its stages. La-Charité-sur-Loire has, both in its tower and in the triforium of its choir, foliated semi-circular arches—but in this case cinquefoil. The trefoiled arch gives something of a Moorish look to the buildings where it is employed, especially when it has long drooping cusps as in the examples at Le Puy Cathedral and Issoire.

[1] The four columns supporting the lantern at Ainay are said to have been formed from two real Roman columns taken from an altar, which stood at the meeting of the two great rivers Rhône and Saône near by.

Its affinity, however, is probably rather with the foliated arches that are not an uncommon feature of the Romanesque of the Rhine Provinces and that occur in blank arcading in such churches as the Abbey of Laach or St.-Victor at Xanten.

(B) Buttresses

It is very characteristic of the Romanesque of the country south of the Loire that the buttresses, especially of the apse and of apsidal chapels, take the form of classical columns with carved Corinthianesque capitals. It is as though the columns which adorn the Roman triumphal arches, as at Orange, Autun and Reims, were understood as buttresses and copied accordingly. Tall clusters of similar columns commonly also act as buttresses of the ornate façades of the Romanesque of the south, dividing the front vertically into three (generally), but sometimes into a larger number of compartments. The use of the columnar buttress is well illustrated in the following examples :

Allier : St.-Menoux.
Aude : Alet.
Corrèze : Brive.
Cher : Blet and Les-Aix-d'Angillon.
Charente : Archingeay and Moutiers-sur-Boëme.
Charente-Inférieure : Échillais, Esnandes, Rétaux, Rioux and Surgères.
Deux-Sèvres : Airvault, St.-Hilaire and St.-Pierre at Melle, and St.-Jouin-de-Marnes.
Gironde : Avensan, Bouliac, Bégadan, Gaillan, Pujols, and St.-André-de-Cubzac.
Hte.-Vienne : Solignac.
Indre : Fontgombault.
Maine-et-Loire : Fontevrault and Savennières.
Puy-de-Dôme : Chamalières, Notre-Dame-du-Port Clermont-Ferrand and Issoire.
Vendée : Vouvant.
Vienne : Lusignan, Montierneuf Poitiers, and St.-Maurice.

In France the fashion of the columnar buttress persisted occasionally in the Transition to Pointed style, as at Noyon Cathedral and even in some churches of the Gothic style as at St.-Paul-Serge Narbonne (Aude), but in the Romanesque of Normandy and the north the buttress takes the form of a flat projection, being little more than a slight thickening of the wall of the structure at the point where extra strength was needed. The churches of Caen, St.-Georges-de-Boscherville, Graville-Ste.-Honorine (Seine-Inférieure) and the Romanesque churches of Calvados in general have the flat "Norman" buttresses with which we are familiar in England in such churches as Iffley (Oxon), Stewkley(Bucks) or old Shoreham (Sussex). The columnar buttress is very rare in English churches, but we meet with it at Berkswell (Warwick), in the chancel of Hanslope (Bucks) and at the angles of the tower of St. Peter's Northampton.

(C) Capitals

In the capitals, especially of the southern Romanesque, is an extraordinary wealth of sculpture, and in some cases, especially in the churches of Auvergne, the carved capitals form almost the sole adornment of the interior of the church.

(1) In some capitals of a *very early type* there is either a rude incised pattern in the form of a sort of volute, as at the ruined church of St.-Martin-du-Canigou Casteil (Pyrénées-Orientales), or sometimes simple attempts at foliage or figure-sculpture in low relief. St.-Savin (Haute-Pyrénées) has rudely shaped capitals with sprays of stiff conventional foliage and figures of heads and animals with stars as disconnected items upon the surface. At Cruas (Ardèche) are similar capitals with grotesque monsters in low relief who carry a second head upon the end of their tails.

(2) In some cases the capitals have an altogether *classic form* as at St.-Hilaire Poitiers, at St.-Aignan-sur-Cher, where we have large capitals with volutes, and at Selles-sur-Cher (Loir-et-Cher), where there is a series of graceful capitals with deeply undercut acanthus and other foliage.

(3) Capitals *adorned with foliage* in very bold relief are frequent, and some of the best examples may be seen at:

Le Puy Cathedral—acanthus, rosettes and human heads.

The cloister of Vaison-la-Romaine (Vaucluse)—foliage with interlacing stalks in high relief.

Aix (Bouches-du-Rhône).

Lesterps (Charente)—an array of pine-cones within a series of diminutive arcades.

The cloister of Moissac (Tarn-et-Garonne).

Hagetmau and St.-Sever (Landes).

Lescar (Basses-Pyrénées).

St.-Benoît-sur-Loire (Loiret)—large capitals in the open portico at the west end.

St.-Genou (Indre).

(4) A *basket-work pattern* of interlacing strands seems to be reminiscent of Byzantine design as seen at Ravenna and occurs in fine capitals at St.-Bertrand-de-Comminges (Hte.-Garonne) in the cloister and also in the cloister at St.-Lizier-de-Couserans (Ariège).

(5) As examples of *figure sculpture* very often mingled with elaborate foliage, the whole in high relief, the following examples may be especially referred to:

Boule-d'Amont (Pyrénées-Orientales).

The cloister at St.-Trophime Arles (Bouches-du-Rhône).

The cloister at Elne (Pyrénées-Orientales), the pillars in this case being very finely diapered.

Hagetmau (Landes).

St.-Aubin Angers.

The church of Ronceray, Angers, with the addition of marked volutes.

St.-Denis Amboise (Indre-et-Loire).

St.-Genou (Indre)—a very splendid series of deep capitals both in the nave arcade and in the triforium above.

Sometimes the figures upon capitals are not isolated, but scenes, either scriptural or from the lives of the Saints, are depicted, as at St.-Eutrope Saintes (Charente-Inférieure), Lesterps (Charente), Moissac (Tarn - et - Garonne), the priory of St.-Léonard at L'île-Bouchard (Indre-et-Loire), Vézelay (Yonne) and at Lescar (Basses-Pyrénées). In the last-named the Fall and theExpulsion from Paradise are vividly portrayed and at St.-Pierre Chauvigny (Vienne) the story of the Nativity is similarly set forth. Monsters, birds and foliage are often mingled together as at Trucy (Aisne) and in the churches of Ste.-Croix and St.-Quiriace at Provins (Seine-et-Marne). Struggles between creatures are depicted, as at La-Charité-sur-Loire, or contests between men and between men and monsters, as at Vézelay. In Auvergne very fine deep capitals with figure sculpture are found especially upon the capitals of the choir and those that bear the narrow stilted arches of the apse, as at Issoire and St.-Nectaire (Puy-de-Dôme).

In their sculptured capitals especially these old churches seem to reach back to a very distant age, a dim and fearful world, of which comparatively few clues remain. The mysterious and baleful creatures that contend with one another, or with man, and that are seen grinning and mocking amongst the figures of stocky saints or angels seem to have materialised out of some vision of fierce temptation, such as those of the hermits, who in the desert contended with the demons of the pit.

(D) PORTALS

Everywhere it was upon the portals of the Romanesque churches that the greatest wealth of ornament was lavished.

The great majority of these doorways are ROUND-HEADED.

(1) It is also characteristic of early Romanesque doorways that they have a horizontal lintel, so that there is a solid *tympanum* above this contained by the semi-circular arch above, the blank space of the tympanum affording opportunity for figure sculpture such as the early builders were wont to use for adornment. The great doorway forming the entrance to a church is often divided in the centre by a pillar, so that under the one arch is a double opening.

Grand examples of such double doorways occur at :

St.-Gilles-du-Gard (Gard).
Riom (Puy-de-Dôme).
Arles (Bouches-du-Rhône).
Ste.-Marthe Tarascon (Bouches-du-Rhône).
Vouvant (Vendée).
Beaulieu (Corrèze).
Conques (Aveyron).
Oloron-Ste.-Marie (Basses-Pyrénées).
St.-Nazaire Carcassonne (Aude).
Morlaas (Basses-Pyrénées).
St.-Bertrand-de-Comminges (Hte.-Garonne).
Moissac (Tarn-et-Garonne).
Caen, Abbaye-aux-Dames.
Bourges Cathedral, south door.
Cahors Cathedral.
The Madeleine Vézelay (Yonne). Two splendid examples, one opening into the narthex and a second from the narthex into the nave.

A favourite subject for the sculpture in the tympanum is Christ seated in glory surrounded by the four symbolical winged creatures of the Apocalypse, as at St.-Gilles-du-Gard, St.-Trophime Arles, Çivray (Vienne), St.-Savin and Luz-St.-Sauveur (Hautes-Pyrénées), Embrun Cathedral (Hautes-Alpes), Maguelone (Hérault), the west doorways of the Cathedrals of Angers and Chartres and the south doorways of Le Mans and Bourges. Of great interest is the vivid portrayal of the Massacre of the Innocents and the Flight into Egypt upon the tympanum of the grand west doorway of the little church at Morlaas (Basses-Pyrénées).

The arches of these portals usually show elaborate figure sculpture or other rich ornament, as at :

St.-Gabriel Tarascon (Bouches-du-Rhône).
Civray (Vienne).
Vouvant (Vendée).
Angoulême Cathedral.
Lichères (Charente).
Champagne-Monton (Charente).
Beaulieu (Corrèze).
St.-Seurin Bordeaux.
La-Lande-de-Cubzac (Gironde).
Conques (Aveyron).
Oloron-Ste.-Marie (Basses-Pyrénées).
Sauveterre-de-Béarn (Basses-Pyr.).
Morlaas (Basses-Pyr.).
Arudy (Basses-Pyr.).
St.-Michel Le Puy.
St.-Bertrand-de-Comminges (Hte.-Garonne).
Moissac (Tarn-et-Garonne).
St.-Denis (Seine).
St.-Étienne Beauvais.
Château-Gontier (Mayenne).
Le Mans—the south door.
Bellegarde (Loiret).
Bourges—the south door.
Cahors Cathedral—north door.
La-Charité-sur-Loire (Nièvre).
Charlieu (Loire).
Langres Cathedral—north door.
St.-Lazare Avallon (Yonne).
Vézelay (Yonne).
Maguelone (Hérault).
Ganagobie (Basses-Alpes).
Esnandes (Charente-Inférieure).
Pont-l'Abbé-d'Arnoult (Ch.-Inf.).
Mimizan (Landes).
Vailly-sur-Aisne (Aisne).

and the west doorways at the Cathedrals of Angers and Chartres.

A subject sometimes treated round the great arch of a portal is the adoration of the four-and-twenty Elders around the throne as seen in the vision of St. John in the Apocalypse. We find this in the doorways at Oloron-Ste.-Marie (Basses-Pyrénées) and at Morlaas in the same Department, and we meet with it again at St.-Pierre-d'Airvault (Deux-Sèvres).

In some of the splendid doorways the openings are flanked by statues, as at St.-Gilles-du-Gard, St.-Trophime Arles, Notre-Dame-du-Port Clermont-Ferrand, Valcabrère (Hte.-Garonne) and in the cathedral doorways at Angers, Le Mans, Chartres and Bourges, where they stand upon and in front of richly diapered pillars. In all these details of the horizontal lintel and tympanum, the double doorway, the figure sculpture in the arches and the flanking figures of saints and kings and symbolic personages, these wonderful portals of the Romanesque churches set a fashion which persisted all through the subsequent Gothic development in France.[1]

In other examples of Romanesque doorways with tympanum the arches are moulded after the fashion which became the usual one in northern Romanesque. We see this treatment in such examples as the following :

Villefranche-de-Conflent (Pyrénées-Orientales), where a cable moulding occurs.
Valcabrère (Hte.-Garonne).
Riom (Puy-de-Dôme).
Digne (Basses-Alpes).
Ste.-Marthe, Tarascon.
Moirax (Lot-et-Garonne).
St.-Savin (Hautes-Pyrénées).
St.-Sever-sur-l'Adour (Landes).
Luz - St.-Sauveur (Hautes-Pyrénées).
St.-Nazaire Carcassonne.
Beost (Basses-Pyrénées).
La Bénissons-Dieu (Loire), with cable moulding.
Donnemarie-en-Montois (Seine-et-Marne).
La Roe (Mayenne).
Le Mans Cathedral—west door.
The two great Abbeys of Caen.
Ouistreham (Calvados).
Colombelles (Calvados).
Mouen (Calvados).
Tour (Calvados).
Ryes (Calvados).
Fontenailles (Calvados).
St.-Loup (Calvados).
The last seven showing with many others in the district, the zigzag moulding that is so frequent in Norman work in England.

Of these doorways with tympanum treated above some are pointed—Maguelone (Hérault), Ganagobie (Basses-Alpes), Esnandes and Pont-l'Abbé-d'Arnoult (Charente-Inférieure), Mimizan (Landes), Vailly-sur-Aisne (Aisne) and the west doorways of Angers and Chartres Cathedrals. To these we may add the example at St.-Pierre Soissons (Aisne). The portal of Embrun is peculiar in being treated altogether after the Italian manner with slender detached pillars resting upon lions. Both in this case and at Cahors Cathedral we find a mingling of round and pointed arches in the

[1] In England the horizontal lintel and tympanum did not survive the Norman style, and double doorways, except in cathedrals and collegiate churches, are rare, though examples occur in the early English style at West Walton (Norfolk) and Higham Ferrers (Northants), and in the Perpendicular style at Edington (Wilts), St. Nicholas King's Lynn and at Lydd and Tenterden (Kent)—all Western doorways.

portals. The doorway at Étoile (Drôme) is singular in having its arch cusped and that of Ganagobie (Basses-Alpes) is scalloped.

(2) A very large number of Romanesque doorways throughout France are *without tympanum* and in some-districts, particularly in the style of Poitou and Saintonge the portals are usually of this kind.

ÉCHILLAIS (CHARENTE-INFÉRIEURE).

Elaborately adorned doorways of this class occur at :

Lescure (Tarn).
St.-Maurice (Vienne).
St.-Jouin-de-Marnes (Deux-Sèvres).
Foussais (Vendée).
Ste.-Croix Bordeaux.
Maillezais (Vendée).
Maillé (Vendée).
Pressac (Vienne).
Melle (Deux-Sèvres).
St.-Pierre-d'Airvault (Deux Sèvres).
Blasimont (Gironde).
Chênehutte-les-Tuffeaux (Maine-et-Loire).
Notre-Dame-la-Grande Poitiers.

Figure sculpture also appears in the arches of the doorways at:

Bournand (Vienne).
Parthenay (Deux-Sèvres).
Argenton-Château (Deux-Sèvres).
St.-Basil Étampes (Seine-et-Oise).
Loches (Indre-et-Loire).

But it is in the Charente district especially that

almost every village church has a deeply recessed portal whose arches are enriched with sculptured foliage of every kind, together with figure sculpture in many

Écurat (Charente-Inférieure).

cases. The following examples are especially worthy of attention :

In Charente-Inférieure :
- Surgères.
- Échillais
- St.-Gemme.
- Chadenac.
- Écoyeux.
- Avy.
- Nieul-lès-Saintes.
- Écurat.
- Le Douhet.
- La Jarrie.
- Jazennes.
- Médis.
- The Abbaye-aux-Dames Saintes.
- Talmont.
- Fénioux.
- Aulnay.
- Ars-en-Ré.

In Charente :
- Trois Palais.
- St.-Amand-de-Boixe.
- Ruffec.
- Chalais.
- Cognac.
- Châteauneuf-sur-Charente.

Other examples have moulded arches and may be classed rather with the type of Romanesque of Normandy and the north, such as :

Montsannes (Haute-Garonne).
Jazneuil (Vienne).
Oulmes (Vendée), with moulding of tooth-ornament.
Plassac (Charente).
La Péruse (Charente).
Confolens (Charente).
Bois (Charente).
La-Chaize-Giraud (Vendée) has cable moulding.
Ste.-Croix Oloron (Basses-Pyrénées)
Brioude (Hte.-Loire).
Vieille Brioude (Hte.-Loire).
St.-Volusien Foix (Ariège).
Les Baux (Bouches-du-Rhône).
St.-Gilles Étampes (Seine-et-Oise).
Ruan (Loir-et-Cher).
Ygrandes (Allier).
Til-Châtel (Côte-d'Or).
St.-Georges-d'Oléron (Charente-Inférieure).

There is a remarkable small group of doorways in the western part of central France, in which a series of recessed wavy mouldings enclose the doorway without other ornament and without the usual lateral pillars and capitals. Portals of this unusual and striking design occur at Le Dorat (Hte.-Vienne), La Souterraine (Creuse) and in the transept at Vigeois (Corrèze). In the two last the doorway itself is cusped, but at Le Dorat the large containing arch encloses two separate pointed entrances. The doorways at Le Dorat and La Souterraine open into a western narthex-tower with subsidiary turrets at the north and south ends of its base. By a Limousin localism the great doorways are flanked on either side by a deep, tall and very narrow recess. St.-Junien (Hte.-Vienne) has a similar arrangement of its west façade. Other cusped doorways occur at Chalais (Charente) and Petit-Palais (Gironde), while at Surgères (Charente-Inférieure) and at the chapel of St.-Crépin Evron (Mayenne) the arches of doorways have a still more unusual scalloped outline.

In comparatively few cases the recessed arches of portals are quite plain, as at Bussières-Badil and St.-Privat (Dordogne), Garchizy (Nièvre), Fontevrault (Maine-et-Loire) and Le-Mas-d'Agenais (Lot-et-Garonne), the last-named being also without the usual lateral shafts.

As one moves northward moulded arches become more

common instead of richly adorned ones as at Nieul-sur-l'Autize (Vendée), St.-Benoît (Vienne), Meung (Loiret), St.-Pierre Saumur (Maine-et-Loire), and St.-André Chartres; and when we come to Normandy moulded arches are the rule, generally adorned with zigzag, as at Formigny, St.-Pierre-sur-Dives, Carpiquet, Cintheaux, Biéville and Thaon (Calvados), or occasionally with the beak-head ornament as at Auvillars (Calvados), both of which are familiar to those who know the Norman churches of England. At Mortain (Manche) is a fine doorway surrounded by zigzag mouldings which run down to the bottom on either side without interruption —there being no lateral shafts—as in the case of the west door at Iffley (Oxon).

The vast majority of Romanesque doorways without tympanum are round-headed, but here and there we find them pointed, as in the examples at Argenton-Château (Deux-Sèvres), La-Chaize-Giraud, Maillé and Maillezais (Vendée), Ars-en-Ré and St.-Georges-d'Oléron (Charente-Inférieure) and the chapel of St.-Crépin at Evron (Mayenne). Pointed and round forms of arch are mixed at Valréas (Vaucluse), Notre-Dame-la-Grande Poitiers, Pressac (Vienne), St. Pierre-d'Airvault and Melle (Deux Sèvres), Échebrune (Charente-Inférieure), Courcome (Charente) and Blasimont (Gironde).

Before we leave the subject of Romanesque portals something must be said as to arrangement and grouping of doorways in a façade. The doorway is usually in the central one of a range of three arches which are all richly adorned and which occupy the ground story of the façade, the lateral arches being generally narrower than the central one, the arrangement being similar to that at the west end of Rochester Cathedral and in the smaller churches at Iffley (Oxon) and Portchester (Hants) in England.

The doorway thus stands in the centre of a range of three arches at :

Esnandes (Charente-Inférieure).
Avy (Charente-Inférieure).
Échebrune (Charente-Inférieure).
Échillais (Charente-Inférieure).
Chadenac (Charente-Inférieure).
Écoyeux (Charente-Inférieure).
Écurat (Charente-Inférieure).
Le Douhet (Charente-Inférieure).
Talmont (Charente-Inférieure).
The Abbaye-aux-Dames Saintes (Charente-Inférieure).
Médis (Charente-Inférieure).
Jazennes (Charente-Inférieure).
Pont-l'Abbe-d'Arnoult (Charente-Inférieure).
La-Chaize-Giraud (Vendée).
Nieul-sur-l'Autize (Vendée).
Foussais (Vendée).
Maillezais (Vendée).
Maillé (Vendée).
Airvault (Deux Sèvres).
Le Mans Cathedral—west door.
Plassac (Charente).
St.-Amand-de-Boixe (Charente).
Ruffec (Charente).
Gensac-la-Pallud (Charente).
Cognac (Charente).
Châteauneuf-sur-Charente (Charente).
La Péruse (Charente).
Bois (Charente).
St. Martin-d'Ary (Charente).
Courcome (Charente).
Çivray (Vienne).
Notre-Dame-la-Grande (Poitiers).
St.-Privat (Dordogne).
Petit-Palais (Gironde).
Blasimont (Gironde).
Ste.-Croix Bordeaux.
St.-Seurin Bordeaux.
Valréas (Vaucluse).
Trie-Château (Oise).
St.-André Chartres.
Tavant (Indre).
Parçay-sur-Vienne (Indre).

At Chartres Cathedral and at St.-Jouin-de-Marnes (Deux-Sèvres) three doorways occupy the lowest stage of the façade, while at Angoulême Cathedral and at St. Paul-de-Varax (Ain), the central arch of a range of five is pierced for the doorway. The very splendid façade at Surgères (Charente-Inférieure) has a range of no less than seven arches, three of which contain doorways, but one of the lateral doorways is now filled with masonry. St.-Gilles-du-Gard is exceptional in having the wall spaces between its three portals covered with fluted pilasters and statuary in front of which stand very graceful columns carrying an elaborately carved frieze.

(E) Towers

In the Romanesque of the south the central tower is the rule, but lateral towers are not uncommon and western towers not infrequently occur. [In the detailed descriptions below Ax denotes axial towers, C indicates a central tower, L a lateral and W a western one.] After the example set in the early church of St.-Martin d'Ainay Lyon several churches have a western as well as a central tower. The important instances of this axial arrangement of towers are: Avignon Cathedral, Cruas (Ardèche), Oloron-Ste.-Marie (Basses-Pyrénées), Le Dorat (Hte.-Vienne), Maillezais and Nieul-sur-l'Autize (Vendée), and the typical churches of Auvergne, such as Issoire, Brioude and Notre-Dame-du-Port Clermont-Ferrand. Among the Auvergne churches, however, Mauriac and St.-Nectaire depart from this arrangement, and substituting two western towers for the common single one of the district, present with the church of Conques (Aveyron) the unusual plan of a three-towered church in the Romanesque of the south.

Over a wide extent of southern France the early towers are severe and plain. Some typical examples may be quoted:

L. Guitres (Gironde), an oblong tower with plain openings in two stages.
L. St. Grégoire Villemagne (Hérault), with two stages of openings.
L. Unac (Ariège), tall and plain with coupled lights.
L. St.-Papoul (Aude), tall with three stages of openings.
W. Ibos (Htes.-Pyrénées), with tall rectangular buttresses.
W. St.-Avit-Sénieur (Dordogne). A pair of towers very severe with tall arcading on the west face.
Ax. Champdieu (Loire).

The usual finish is a low pyramidal cap, and very frequently this cap cuts off the lights at the top of the tower, the masonry of the tower being unfinished, as in examples at:

TOURNUS.

BURGUNDIAN ROMANESQUE.

W. PORTAL, ST.-RICQUIER (SOMME)

FLAMBOYANT.

facing p. 80.

L. Malemort (Corrèze).
L. Ayen (Corrèze).
L. St.-André-de-Cubzac (Gironde).
C. St.-Denis-de-Piles (Gironde).
C. Monsempron (Lot-et-Garonne), tall and very plain.
C. Varen (Tarn-et-Garonne), with flat buttresses.
L. Montpezat-de-Quercy (Tarn-et-Garonne).
L. Unac (Ariège).
Ax. Oloron-Ste.-Marie (Basses Pyrénées), both towers.

Pinnacles and buttresses are generally absent. The church of Ainay at Lyon, however, has heavy ear-like *acrotères* at each corner of the western tower, flanking its blunt spire. The effect of these is very curious and we have similar examples in the Cathedral tower of Embrun at Vallouise and Guillestre (Htes.-Alpes) and at Avensan (Gironde): in the last these curious triangular projections are crowned with small statues. At Ste.-Radegonde Poitiers smaller *acrotères* flank the upper octagon stage of the west tower. The great majority of towers are unbuttressed and where buttresses occur, they often take the form of clusters of columns. Examples will be noted below. Occasionally a tower is battlemented as at St.-Martin-du-Canigou Casteil and Elne (Pyrénées-Orientales), the latter very tall and arcaded in four stages.[1] Both these are west towers. Other interesting west towers are at Chantemerle (Drôme) with coupled belfry lights divided by a shaft and an ancient one at Aire-sur-l'Adour (Landes) with primitive masonry and arches of mingled straight-sided and semicircular shapes, such as distinguish early structures elsewhere in examples like the baptistery of St.-Jean at Poitiers and the church of St.-Généroux (Vienne).

A curious tower is the oblong one at the end of the south transept at St.-Chef (Isère) and still more strange are the two apparent cases of a tower at the east end.

[1] See below on fortified churches, p. 214.

At Vénerque (Hte.-Garonne) the polygonal apse has been fortified, its walls being carried up above the chancel roof and battlemented, so that it has the look of a tower. Even more remarkable is the strange planning of the church at Les-Saintes-Maries (Bouches-du-Rhône), where the special chapel containing the shrine and relics of the patron saints has been built above the apse of the strongly fortified church,[1] so that the east end towers above the rest of the building.

A few towers towards the south-east, such as St.-Pierre Vienne, Embrun Cathedral and Guillestre (Htes.-Alpes) have openings in their successive stages in the Italian manner, the lights increasing in number in each stage as the tower mounts upwards. The graceful circular "Tour Fenestrelle," flanking the former Cathedral of Uzès (Gard) and dating from the twelfth century, also has affinity rather with the Italian campanile than with the French Romanesque belfry and recalls the famous tower of Pisa.

We also meet with towers which have somewhat shallow surface arcading, similar to that which is found on Norman towers in England, as at Vieux-Pouzauges (Vendée), Le Dorat and St.-Léonard (Hte.-Vienne) and St.-Salvi at Albi (Tarn). But more usually the tower is covered with arcading, or in some cases may be said to consist of piled-up stages of arcading, and this, especially in Poitou and Saintonge, has well-formed shafts and deeply-moulded arches, some of which are

[1] The usual position for the shrine of a patron saint is in a crypt below the apse, where in early times the bodies and relics of the saints were deposited, and the technical name of which was the *Confessio.* The shrine of St.-Germanus is in this position at St.-Germain Auxerre, and a crypt of the kind remains in the Saxon chancel at Wing (Bucks) in England. Sometimes in France, as at Ste.-Radegonde Poitiers and at Vouvant (Vendée), the chamber containing the shrine has an open arch to the nave, and the raised chancel above it is approached by steps on either side.

pierced for lights. Fine examples of arcaded towers occur at:

W. St.-Porchaire Poitiers.
W. St.-Seurin Bordeaux. This church has a little duplicate of its tower on the south side of the nave, for a clock-tower.
W. Ste.-Croix Bordeaux. A pair of towers.
Tr. Angoulême Cathedral. A lofty tower over the north transept, one of an intended pair.
C. Notre-Dame-la-Grande Poitiers. Round upon a square base.
C. Lusignan (Vienne).
C. Lencloitre (Vienne).
C. St.-Pierre Melle (Deux-Sèvres).
C. Parthenay-le-Vieux (Deux-Sèvres). Octagonal with a light in each face.
C. Marnes (Deux-Sèvres). With very narrow lights.
C. Oulmes (Vendée).
C. Rétaux (Charente-Inférieure). Octagonal with narrow lights on each face.
C. Thézac (Charente-Inférieure).
C. Courcome and St.-Amand-de-Boixe (Charente).
C. Mouthiers-sur-Boëme (Charente). Octagonal with a light on each face.
C. Aubazine (Corrèze). Octagonal on a square base.
C. St.-Robert (Corrèze). Octagonal.
C. Gaillan (Gironde).
C. Bussières-Badil (Dordogne). A very low octagon with lights on each face.
C. Livernon (Lot).
C. Maubourget (Htes.-Pyrénées). An octagon with lights on each face.
C. St.-Savin (Htes.-Pyrénées). Octagonal.
C. Sauveterre (Basses-Pyrénées).
C. L'Hôpital-St.-Blaise (Basses-Pyrénées). Octagonal.
C. St.-Lizier-de-Couserans (Ariège). With straight-sided arches.
C. St.-Sernin Toulouse. A very lofty octagonal tower of five stages. The three lower stages have round arches, and the two upper ones the straight-sided arches that are frequent in the brick architecture of the district.
C. Rieux-Minervois (Aude). A plain unfinished octagon.
C. St.-Martin-de-Londres (Hérault). A low octagon.
C. Bénévent-l'Abbaye (Creuse). An octagon with lights on each face.
C. Chambon (Creuse). With coupled lights.
C. Cavaillon (Vaucluse). An octagon with lights on each face.
C. St.-Honorat Arles (Bouches-du-Rhône). An octagon of two stages of open arches.

The central octagons of the churches of Auvergne have lights on each face, as at La Bourboule (Puy-de-Dôme), Brioude (Hte.-Loire) and La Garde-Adhémar (Drôme), and these are coupled with a central shaft at Issoire, Riom, St.-Saturnin, St.-Nectaire, Notre-Dame-du-Port Clermont-Ferrand (Puy-de-Dôme) and Mauriac (Cantal).

The usual finish of the Romanesque towers of the south is a blunt four-sided pyramid, but in the west, especially in the Charente district, short stone spires occur :

C. Melleran (Deux-Sèvres).
L. Fénioux (Charente-Inférieure).
C. Trois-Palais, Plassac, Gensac, St.-Estèphe (Charente). Of these Gensac has angle pinnacles and grouped belfry-lights in the tower.
L. Bassac (Charente).
W. Avensan (Gironde). A square spire. The belfry lights are grouped.
L. Loupiac (Gironde). The belfry lights are grouped. Angle pinnacles stand upon small shafts and there is a light at the base of the spire.
C. Aillas (Gironde).
C. Bourg-St.-Andéol (Ardèche). The spire has lights of triangular shape.

The design of the central octagon at Surgères (Charente-Inférieure) is exceptional. It consists entirely of groups of shafts with narrow slits between for lights. This tower has, like that of St.-Seurin Bordeaux, a little replica of itself for a clock-tower, set on the north side of the nave.

Notre-Dame-la-Grande Poitiers has a short conical spire covered with a scaly pattern giving it a pine-cone appearance, and the two flanking turrets of the west façade are similarly capped. Spires of this pine-cone pattern occur elsewhere, as at Couronne, Bassac, Plassac, and St.-Estèphe (Charente), Fénioux, the Abbaye-aux-Dames Saintes and the little clock-tower at Surgères (Charente-Inférieure). The domes at the Cathedrals of Angoulême and Périgueux are similarly covered with scaly pattern. The upper part of these towers is often of circular plan, as in the examples at Notre-Dame-la-Grande Poitiers, the Abbaye-aux-Dames Saintes and Fénioux. The central tower at Cruas

Couronne (Charente).

(Ardèche), after a short octagonal stage upon a square base, rises for two finely-designed stages in circular form, but towers round from their base are rare in France. The only instances are the very graceful campanile of

St.-Théodorat at Uzès (Gard) and the much plainer. though equally Italian-looking, tower of the Chapelle-Santa-Colonna in Andorre.

Where buttresses occur in these towers of the south they are frequently formed of clusters of columns, like the buttresses of façades, as at St.-Porchaire Poitiers,

SOULOM (HAUTES-PYRÉNÉES).

Ste.-Croix Bordeaux, Gensac (Charente), Lencloitre (Vienne) and St.-Pierre Melle (Deux-Sèvres).

A good many churches of the south are towerless, particularly towards the mountainous districts of the Alps and the Pyrénées. The church bells are then usually hung in bell-gables as at Planès (Pyrénées-Orientales), Tarascon-sur-Ariège (Ariège) and Celleneuve (Hérault), and frequently in such gables there are two tiers of bells as at Ste.-Léocadie, Ourjout, Orlu (Ariège) and Ydes (Cantal). At Lannes (Lot-et-Garonne) is a very tall gable with three tiers of openings. In a few cases openings are somewhat strangely made for the

Gotein (Basses-Pyrénées).

bells in the western gable of the nave, as at Blasimont and Savignac (Gironde) and Morlaas (Basses-Pyrénées). A not uncommon arrangement is to raise a strip of wall in openings in which the bells are hung, as at the church of St.-Valier St.-Girons and Verdun (Ariège), Moirax (Lot-et-Garonne), and Le Pujol (Hérault). An oblong belfry of this kind sometimes has a gabled roof with projecting eaves, making a picturesque feature, as at Espalion (Aveyron) and Soulom (Htes.-Pyrénées). In the Pyrénées a small gable sometimes has a wooden cage behind it for the bells and is machicolated in front, as at Bidart and Guéthary (Basses-Pyrénées), or a tall wall gabled at the top masks a wooden structure for the bells, as in the church in the lower town at Lescar (Basses-Pyrénées). Another strictly local fashion characteristic of the same district is a range of three tall and sharply pointed gables at the west end, winning for the class of churches that possess them the name of *Églises Trinitaires*. There are typical examples at Ascain and Gotein (Basses-Pyrénées), and at the very curious church of Aussurucq, in the same Department, a high wall at the west, terminating in three points, has a wooden structure for bells on either side of it.

In the south it is also customary to hang bells externally in a frame or cage of wrought iron which sometimes becomes an ornamental feature through its intricate design. There are many instances in Spain, especially in Catalonia, as at the Cathedral and University of Barcelona, and we find a good many examples in France :

Perpignan Cathedral (Pyrénées-Orientales).
Clermont-l'Hérault and Béziers Cathedral (Hérault).
Bourg-St.-Audéol (Ardèche).
Courpière and the Sainte-Chapelle at Riom (Puy-de-Dôme).
Semur-en-Auxois (Côte-d'Or).
Crest and Die (Drôme).
Vaison Cathedral (Vaucluse).
Digne Cathedral (Basses-Alpes).
Le-Cannet-du-Lac (Var).
St.-Paul-Serge Narbonne (Aude).
St.-Gilles (Gard).
Château-Gombert, St.-Esprit Aix, Les Martigues and Grans (Bouches-du-Rhône).

The Hôtels-de-Ville at Aix-en-Provence and Tarascon have similar bell-cages as has the Tour de-l'Horloge at Apt (Vaucluse), and an elaborate iron frame for the bell surmounts the great square tower of the Comtes - de - Toulouse which dominates the curious little town of Pernes (Vaucluse). Farther north is a very notable example at Notre-Dame Dijon, where there is, above the west façade, an elaborate bell-cage with attendant figures of Jacquemard de Courtrai, his wife and children.

Bell-Cage, Perpignan Cathedral.

As we go northwards into Burgundy Romanesque towers are not so frequent. There are, however, three splendid examples of churches of the three-towered plan. Tournus (Saône-et-Loire) has a tall central tower, square and beautifully arcaded, with a similarly designed one, of smaller dimensions, on the north side of the western narthex. The fellow-tower to the south has never been carried up, and terminates in a gabled finish, perhaps showing the original design of the pair of towers at the west end of this church. At Paray-le-Monial (Saône-et-Loire) is a large and tall central octagon, and a pair of western towers, graceful and slight in their proportions, with three tiers of typical Romanesque lights. La-Charité-sur-Loire has kept intact its low central octagon and its very tall and beautiful north-west tower with two upper stages of three coupled lights on each face, but the corresponding south-west tower has shared in the ruin which has overtaken the greater part of this singularly noble church.

The Department of Allier has some very fine Romanesque central towers at St. Menoux, Veauce, Ygrandes (octagonal), Colombier and Châtel-Montagne. Souvigny in the same Department has at its Abbey Church two short towers at the west end, of good design, and Ébreuil has at its west end an arrangement only paralleled at St.-Benoît-sur-Loire; a large oblong mass with two stages of large and bold arcading, the arches of the upper one being open, stands upon an open portico of three tall arches on its west side and two on the north and south, the east side being formed by the wall of the nave with its main doorway.

There are also notable Romanesque towers at St.-Paul-de-Varax (Ain) and Til-Châtel (Côte-d'Or), both central and very plain, with coupled belfry-lights. Nantua (Ain) has a central octagon. Vermenton (Yonne) has two west towers. The one on the south is, in its upper part, late and poor, but the north tower is of fine Romanesque and retains the lower part of a stone spire, with spire-light, and well-designed angle pinnacles upon diminutive open arches. St.-Germain Auxerre also has a stone spire and the church of St.-Eusèbe in the same city has a very graceful lateral tower, octagonal in its top story and with fine openings in three stages, to which a Gothic spire has been added. At Druyes in the same Department is a plain and massive central tower with coupled belfry lights.

Towards the north-east are fine Romanesque towers at Vertus (Marne)—lateral—Vignory and a central tower at Ceffonds (Hte.-Marne); a fine and massive central tower at Champ-le-Duc and a very curious and heavy oblong narthex-tower at St.-Maurice Épinal (Vosges). Saverne (Bas-Rhin) has a tower of somewhat southern aspect, with receding stages and small belfry lights reminiscent of St.-Trophime Arles.

Passing on to the region of the Loire and beyond into Normandy we come to a district of true spires in the Romanesque style. Just as the pine-cone spires of the Charente district were an application to the tower of the domical roofs of Périgord and Angoumois, so the stone spires of Touraine and Normandy were in their origin an extension of the vaulted roof upwards and are, in fact, not always confined to the tower. In the apse of the church of St.-Nicholas at Caen, in the transept chapel at Audrieu (Calvados)—both Romanesque—as well as in the early Pointed lateral chapels to the lovely choir of Norrey (Calvados) and in the chapels of the *chevet* at Bourges Cathedral, we meet with the stone spire as a roof of some part of the structure other than the tower. But the crowning proof that the spire is only a pointed roof, if further proof were needed, is found at Loches (Indre-et-Loire), where not only the stone capping of the two towers—one central and one western—but also the stone vault of each of the two bays of the nave that lies between them takes the pyramid or spire form and is open to the apex in the interior. The adornment of some early spires with a kind of scaly pattern, as at Notre-Dame Étampes (Seine-et-Oise), or with horizontal ridges as at Bayeux Cathedral and at Tour (Calvados) is evidently a perpetuation in the more durable material of stone of the form of earlier pyramidal tiled roofs.

Many of these early spires are of slight elevation, and being related to the stone vault they do not overhang the tower and have no eaves. Good examples of the type are :

In *Touraine* :

L. Cunault, Trèves (Maine-et-Loire).
C. Ferrière-l'Arcon (Indre-et-Loire).

To these may be added examples farther afield :

C. Jouy-le-Moutier (Seine-et-Oise)
L. Mareil-Marly (Seine-et-Oise).
W. Meung (Loiret).
C. Reilly (Oise).

And an imposing group of three towers at Morienval (Oise), one large tower at the west end and two smaller ones flanking the apse, these last having blunt pyramids of stone.

Some spires are of greater elevation and more graceful proportions :

C. Chemillé (Maine-et-Loire).
C. Cinq-Mars (Indre-et-Loire).
L. Beaulieu-lès-Loches, Courçay, Le Bourgeuil and Rillé (Indre-et-Loire).
W. Langéais (Indre-et-Loire).

To which should be added very fine outlying examples at Notre-Dame Étampes (Seine-et-Oise) and the detached tower at La-Trinité Vendôme (Loir-et-Cher). This last has an octagonal drum upon a square tower, with a lofty spire for finish and in having these three stages resembles the tower at St.-Germain Auxerre.

Pinnacles commonly mark the transition from tower to spire, as at Cunault, Beaulieu-lès-Loches, St.-Martin-de-la-Place, Cinq-Mars, Ferrière-l'Arcon, Meung, Langéais and Rillé, and more fully developed pinnacles in the shape of pyramids upon diminutive shafts at Notre-Dame Étampes and Vendôme.

Spire-lights occur in the cardinal faces of the spire at its base at Beaulieu - lès - Loches, Rillé and in the more elaborate examples at Notre-Dame Étampes and Vendôme, but by a localism in Touraine lights are placed at the base of the spire on the diagonal faces, so as to be a substitute for pinnacles. This curious feature is seen at Le Bourgeuil, Chemillé, Trèves and Courçay. Courçay has the diminishing series of wind-holes which became a feature of Gothic spires later on and is remarkable for its decidedly convex outline; a rather unpleasant peculiarity which it shares with other early spires at Le-

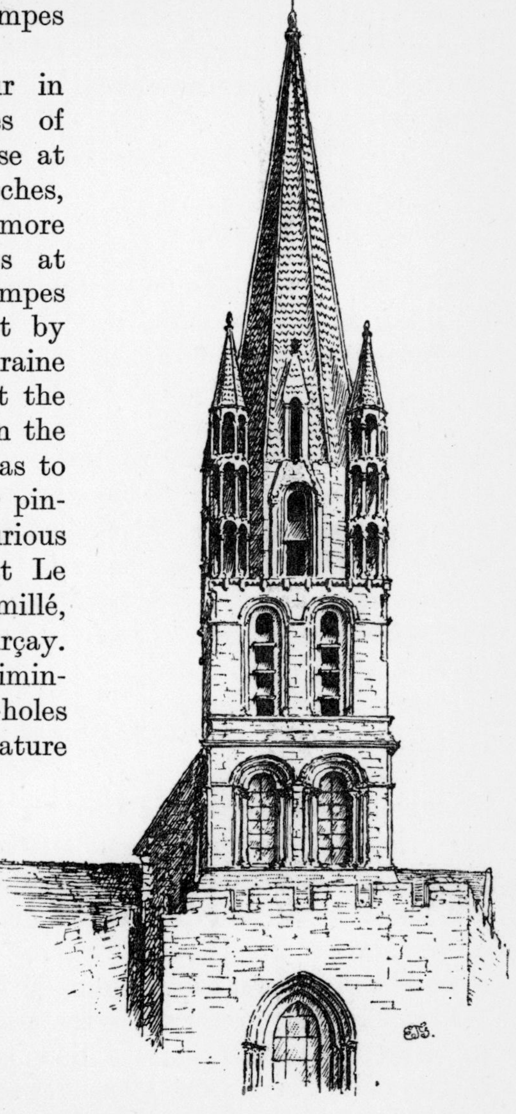

NOTRE-DAME ÉTAMPES (SEINE-ET-OISE).

Puy-Notre-Dame (Maine-et-Loire) and St.-Cirgues and St.-Marie-des-Chazes (Hte.-Loire).

Noteworthy towers without spires in this district are at Fontevrault Abbey and Preuilly (Indre-et-Loire), both unfinished and terminating in a wooden stage and a wonderfully pleasing little lateral tower on a small scale at the church of St.-Laurent Loches.

In *Normandy* :

The early towers of parochial churches are mostly lateral or central and some are crowned by a blunt pyramid of stone which forms the earliest type of Norman spire. Excellent examples are seen at Thaon, Haute-Allemagne, Ver and Rosel (Calvados). The tower at Ver is in receding stages and the short spire at Rosel has lights at its base.

Very pleasing short spires of stone are found at St.-Loup near Bayeux, St.-Michel Vaucelles near Caen, Basly, Cintheaux, Vienne and Colombiers-sur-Seulle—the last named spire having horizontal bands of ornament, a fashion which became permanent locally and lasted on into the Gothic style.

Taller spires occur at Secqueville-en-Bessin and Bény-sur-Mer (both banded and having spire-lights) and Colleville. The top story of the tower at Colleville has two circular openings on each face, a feature also found at Englesqueville. Round openings of the kind became a characteristic of the Anglo-Norman style and are found in England at Old Shoreham (Sussex), East Meon (Hants) and Hemel Hempstead (Herts). Similar openings in increased number became a prominent feature in the greater Norman towers of Ely and Norwich Cathedrals.

Some fine towers in the Department of Calvados have a gabled or saddleback finish, such as Fontenay-le-

Marmion, Longueraye and Parfouru-Léclin.[1] The gabled tower became a great favourite in Normandy, as well as farther north in the district about Soissons and

THE ABBEY OF JUMIÈGES (SEINE-INFÉRIEURE).

outlasted the Romanesque style. There are no less than one hundred and seventy examples in the Depart-

[1] This is a very remarkable tower. It has the receding stages seen elsewhere in Normandy, as at Ver, and in the south at St.-Trophime Arles. Its windows are of a very early type, consisting of small rounded lights separated only by shafts, and its masonry largely consists of herringbone work.

ment of Calvados alone. In the Department of Oise two splendid instances should be specially mentioned—the lofty central tower at Nogent-les-Vierges with two successive stages of bold arcading and a very pleasing central tower at La Villetertre with very long belfry lights and a light above in the centre of a gable with bands of ornament.[1]

Of Norman towers without stone spires we should note those of Lion-sur-Mer, Clinchamps-sur-Orne, St.-Gervais Falaise (a beautiful central tower with long lights), St.-Pierre-sur-Dives (the south-west tower with a later spire of Transitional character), and two good octagonal towers on square bases at Tourdouet and Drubec (Calvados).

Of the great three-towered Norman churches Jumièges is the earliest with square central tower, and lofty west towers surmounted by octagonal drums. The Abbaye aux-Hommes at Caen has a central octagon and two fine western towers with tall spires. The sister foundation of the Abbaye-aux-Dames shows a square central tower and two western towers the upper parts of which have been somewhat roughly treated in the Renaissance period. St.-Pierre at Lisieux also has in its south-west tower a good Romanesque tower within its upper part above the church roof—three stages with two coupled lights on each face. Bayeux Cathedral retains two plain "Norman" towers and spires at its west façade, but the crossing and choir has been remodelled in Gothic.

[1] On gabled towers see further below, pp. 175–180.

BEAUVAIS CATHEDRAL.

facing p. 96.

CHAPTER V

GOTHIC—ITS RISE AND DEVELOPMENT

(1) The Rise of Gothic Architecture

The pointed Gothic style took its rise from the exigencies of vaulting. It resulted from an attempt to provide the most artistic, and at the same time the most economical, solution of the problem of how to erect a fire-proof covering for the intersection of two avenues of different widths, the only material available being stone quarried in small pieces. It was found that while the junction of two barrel-vaults of different widths provided a very awkward problem for the masons, it was comparatively easy to erect a vault over such an intersection, provided that a pointed arch were used, for it is a property of the pointed arch that one can have any number of such forms all sharing the same height from impost to apex, and yet of various widths or spacing at the base. The mediæval builders adopted the pointed arch for constructional reasons, but in the south of France and for some time also in the north, their fashion of building was not affected by this step, the smaller arches of doorways and of windows inserted in the walls retaining their semi-circular heads. Thus we have already found pointed arches supporting the domes of Le Puy Cathedral and of the churches of Périgord, structures which show no approach to a pointed style and seem to have had no influence upon the formation of it.[1]

[1] See above, p. 34.

But the pointed form having been adopted for the main structural arches, the subordinate round-headed arches of windows, doorways or ornamental arcading created a discord and although there was no necessity for the windows to be given pointed arches as well, yet it seemed desirable to the designers on æsthetic grounds to make them conform to the pattern of the vaults. Then, after the features of external walls such as doorways or windows, internal adjuncts like surface arcading, or accessories in the shape of screens and stalls—whether in stone or wood—followed suit and the pointed form of arch became conventional. Such was the origin of the "Gothic" style and its birth and development took place in the Ile-de-France and the gradually extending *Domaine Royale*, with the adjoining territories of Picardy and Champagne, Burgundy forming a sort of secondary centre of influence. The case of Normandy was rather different and will be specially noticed later on.[1]

(2) The Wonderful Development and Widespread Distribution of Gothic

When once the conception of a pointed style was taken up its development as an architectural style was marvellous and its technical development surprisingly swift. It began in the second half of the twelfth century working up from relatively modest beginnings and tentative experiments in churches of Transitional character, as we may call them, such as the Abbey of St.-Denis begun under Abbot Suger 1144, the Cathedrals of Noyon, Senlis and Laon and the collegiate church at Braine (Aisne), the last a little later, towards the close of the twelfth century.

[1] See below, pp. 112–117.

Then followed an increasing magnificence of conception in churches belonging to an early fully-pointed style:

Mantes (Seine-et-Oise), begun towards the close of the twelfth century.
Notre-Dame Paris (end of the twelfth and beginning of the thirteenth centuries), with its severe grandeur.
Chartres, Bourges and Soissons Cathedrals (all begun at the end of the twelfth century).
St.-Léger at Soissons and the choir of St.-Rémi at Reims.
Châlons-sur-Marne Cathedral (of the early thirteenth century).
Culminating in the solemn majesty of the Cathedral of Reims, begun by Jean Orbais in 1212.

Ere the thirteenth century closed the development reached its climax in the evolution of geometrical tracery, as at the Ste.-Chapelle of St.-Louis in Paris (1248), in the serene exaltation of Amiens with its suave and lofty grace, conceived under the architect Robert-de-Luzarches in 1220 and in the vast skyward surge of the vaulting shafts of the choir of Beauvais with its four towering tiers of glazed lights, finished in 1272.

Just as the technical development of Gothic style was amazingly swift, so too its influence was widespread, extending over civilised Europe like a flood. It became the dominant style of northern France and of Belgium and invaded the southern provinces where the Romanesque had its firmly established home. There are Gothic Cathedrals at Aix-en-Provence, Toulouse, Albi, Montpellier, Mende, Clermont-Ferrand, Limoges, Tulle, Rodez, Bazas, Auch and Bayonne.

Important Gothic churches also occur in the south at:

Mirepoix (Ariège).
Carcassonne, St.-Nazaire in the Cité, and St.-Michel and St.-Vincent in the Ville-Basse.
Toulouse.
Gaillac (Tarn).
Clermont-l'Hérault and Béziers (Hérault).
St.-Laurent Le Puy and the Abbey of La-Chaise-Dieu (Hte.-Loire).
Le-Moutier-d'Ahun (Creuse).
St.-Maurice Vienne and St.-Antoine (Isère).
Avignon, St.-Pierre and St.-Agricole.

St.-Pierre and St.-Michel-aux-Lions in Limoges and St.-Yrieix (Hte.-Vienne).
Marmande (Lot-et-Garonne).
The Abbey of Beaulieu, Ginals (Tarn-et-Garonne).
Ligugé (Vienne).
The façades of the cathedral and Ste.-Radegonde at Poitiers.
Bordeaux, a great part of the Cathedral and the church of St.-Michel.
Bazas, Uzeste and the tower and spire at St.-Émilion (Gironde).
Notre-Dame Niort, St.-Maixent, St.-Marc-la-Lande and Bressuire (Deux-Sèvres).
Notre-Dame Fontenay-le-Comte (Vendée).
Marennes, St.-Just, and St.-Pierre and St.-Eutrope at Saintes (Charente-Inférieure).
Larroumieu and Condom (Gers).

The general superiority of the northern French school of architecture found recognition not only in other provinces of France but, either in single buildings or as a prevailing influence, throughout Europe from Silesia to Spain. The Gothic checked the native Romanesque in the Rhine valley and reared the great cathedrals of Strasbourg and Cologne. Elsewhere in Germany churches at Ratisbon, Ulm and Freiburg-im-Breisgau witnessed to its power. It inspired the lofty choir at Utrecht in Holland and in Spain such cathedrals as Burgos, Léon, Oviedo, Toledo and Barcelona. In England the influence of the French Gothic movement is especially seen at Canterbury Cathedral and at Westminster Abbey, apart from the Anglo-Norman development of a transition to pointed style, which led on to the English type of Gothic architecture.[1]

(3) The Special Character of Gothic

This wide appeal of the French Gothic is quite intelligible for two main reasons :

(*a*) In the first place it seems best to correspond with man's ideal conception as to what architecture should be. Structure and ornament appear in their true relation, or rather structure is ornament and ornament

[1] On the Anglo-Norman Gothic, see below, pp. 112–115.

structure. The anatomy of a Gothic church, like that of a human body is all organic with every member an essential part of the life of the whole. To carry on the comparison, a building has its skeleton or structural frame-work, its internal organs and its covering or skin. In different types of architecture the interest is centred on another of these, but in the French Gothic the structural skeleton is made the most of and developed to its logical conclusion and a great church produces its effect by proclaiming its own inner constitution. It stands naked and unashamed, a glorious form resplendent in its purity. For a Gothic church could not be stripped. Other architecture needs clothing with ornament, but Gothic needs no clothes since every part of it has the natural beauty of form which only exists when an object is performing some particular function and is specially adapted to the performance of it. In other architecture the wall does everything, but Gothic in its highest development has no wall, for there is next to no wall in the Cathedrals of Amiens and Beauvais : it raises a soaring creation of buttresses, pinnacles and traceried windows ; it is all organic and athletic ; all ornament and all structure.

(*b*) Another reason for the widespread enthusiasm for Gothic architecture in western Europe from the twelfth to the fifteenth century lies in the fact that—like all the best human art—it was an attempt to express through material means man's inarticulate cravings of the spirit ; to visualise his heavenly dream. Human activities in the domain of art, music or literature are noble because they are efforts, by means of form, colour, sound or words, to express the inexpressible. Faith, the spring of all fine action, is the quality of seeing the invisible. But all material means are inadequate as expressions of spiritual vision, and the Gothic architecture of the Middle Ages accordingly remained ideal in great measure and was not brought to perfection in execution. Few French Gothic churches were actually finished. The wonderful steeple groups its cathedrals were designed to bear were never carried out,[1] and the style culminates in the incomplete cathedral of Beauvais, the great example of what Gothic architecture strove for—the utterance of the unutterable. "Amiens is a giant in repose, Beauvais a tall man on tiptoe"; so runs the oft-quoted epigram. And it hints at the deep truth. Beauvais seems to embody the very genius of Gothic architecture because it is straining after a celestial vision beyond actual sight. It is but a fragment and it may be easy for a critic to point out some of its structural defects, but it has none of the ungainliness of failure and the interior of its *chevet* is of the most satisfying beauty. It strikes one like some great hymn to Heaven suddenly interrupted and rises before the eyes as the very climax of mystic vision caught in visible form. The grandeur of the conception is all the more borne in upon us because the work is unfinished and this is more or less true of Gothic architecture as a whole. The appeal of Gothic architecture may be compared to that of Michael Angelo's statues—most of them unfinished. In one of his Madonnas the feet of the Christ-child are still imprisoned in the clinging marble. The great sculptor was never satisfied with the creations of his mighty genius. His ideals were so high that he could not reach them. He expressed what he could of his splendid vision and there left it. In this he was a true artist, and of all true art Browning's words might serve as a motto:

> . . . A man's reach should exceed his grasp,
> Or what's a Heaven for?

[1] See below, pp. 133, 134.

(4) The Course of Gothic Development in its Plan and Main Features

Fine examples of Transitional churches occur at St.-Germer (Oise) and Pontigny (Yonne), both churches of a severe type with some admixture of round-arched and pointed forms in the single windows. Both are cruciform with aisles to nave and chancel.

Noyon Cathedral is a remarkable instance of early Gothic, and Senlis Cathedral may be classed with it. In both, the apse retains the semi-circular form characteristic of Romanesque churches. At Noyon the leading feature of the plan is its *tri-apsal* character, the transepts as well as the choir terminating in a semi-circular apse. This arrangement may be traced to the ruins of the Roman palace at Trier. It became a favourite plan for the Romanesque churches at Cologne, (Santa-Maria-in-Capitolio, the Apostles' Church and St.-Martin's), and was splendidly carried out at Tournai Cathedral, also in Romanesque. Noyon formed a joint bishopric with Tournai up to about the middle of the twelfth century, and this would account for the adoption of the semi-circular apse for the transepts as well as for the choir at Noyon.[1] At Soissons Cathedral the south transept, also of early Gothic, is semi-circular on the ground plan and is a beautiful work, alike finished and refined. In its interior there are four airy stages superimposed, of pointed openings arranged in bays of triplets with very slender pillars. There is an ambulatory or aisle both at the ground level and at the stage above, each with a chapel projecting towards the east. Occasional examples of apsidal transept also occur

[1] The plan with apses for the transepts as well as for the east end occurs in Italy at Como (the Cathedral and San Fedele), at St.-Peter's Rome and Florence Cathedral. In England St. George's Windsor stands alone in having apsidal transepts, but its east end is rectangular.

elsewhere—in the Romanesque style at St.-Maurice and Gençay (Vienne) and Bayon (Gironde)—in early Gothic at Meung (Loiret)—and Renaissance examples at Vannes Cathedral (Morbihan) and St.-Pierre Douai (Nord).

The Cathedral at Laon is another of the great churches of the north which may be called "Transitional" in character. Its leading feature is its group of seven towers, never completely carried out, but intended to crown the mighty church that surmounts the long precipitous hill-ridge. The east end is rectangular and with its large *rosaçe* reminds one of the east end of Durham Cathedral. About the interior there is an air of great severity, adornment being practically confined to the carved capitals. In this cathedral we note a well-developed western façade with its pair of towers, central *rosaçe* and triple portals below: it is an early example, with the façades at Notre-Dame Mantes (Seine-et-Oise) and Notre-Dame at Paris setting a fashion which was further developed and enriched with statuary at Reims and Amiens, and became thoroughly typical of the Mid-Gothic and the later Gothic churches of France.

At Braisne (Aisne) are the choir and transepts of a remarkable Premonstratensian church, dating from about 1180. In its general features it resembles Laon Cathedral. Its apse is aisleless, and especially pleasing is the very unusual arrangement of semi-circular chapels —a pair on each side—in the angles between the choir and transepts with their axes diagonally to the arms of the cruciform church.

Amongst these early Gothic churches the Cathedral of Sens holds an important place. It still guards amongst its treasures the vestments of St. Thomas of Canterbury, who was in exile here at the very time that the building work was going on under William of Sens

(1160–8), the same William who after the fire at Canterbury in 1174 undertook the rebuilding there. There is, as we should expect, a strong resemblance between Sens and the choir of Canterbury—the same simplicity and breadth, the same arch-mouldings and the main avenue in each case covered by a sexpartite vault. We found the earliest instance of this form of vaulting at the Abbaye-aux-Hommes at Caen, and we come across it now in early Gothic churches on a great scale at the Cathedrals of Laon, Notre-Dame Paris, Bourges, Beauvais and the church of Notre-Dame at Dijon.

Of the great early Gothic churches Chartres belongs to a rather different type. Letters remain (written in 1145) recording the extraordinary enthusiasm and religious fervour which accompanied its erection and brought men from all classes of the community and from far and near to share in the work of building.[1] It was the direct outcome of a religious revival and we may not inaptly term it Petrified Religion and it is noble in architecture, magnificent in sculpture and supreme in stained glass. Its general aspect in the interior affects the beholder as few churches can do, though in detail—save in delicately sculptured parts like the great transept portals—it is inclined to be somewhat rude and heavy, as in its plate-tracery and curious flying buttresses of the nave, which are ponderous and enormously strong.

At Bourges, a remarkable feature of the plan is the omission of the transepts altogether. It is a survival from the earlier Romanesque that the apses at the east are semi-circular. With double aisles along the

[1] The extant letters were written by Abbot Haimon of St.-Pierre-sur-Dives (Calvados) to Tutbury in England, and by Hugh Archbishop of Rouen to Thierry, then Bishop of Amiens.

vast unbroken nave and chancel and sweeping right round the huge apse, this cathedral takes rank amongst the greatest of Gothic churches. The main vault is sharply pointed and in the apse its spandrels are curiously pierced by circular openings. As at Beauvais there is a triforium both in the nave and in its inner aisle.

In the world-famous examples of Reims and Amiens we have the flower of the early Gothic developing into Mid-Gothic in the geometrical tracery of the windows and the *rayonnant* forms of the great *rosaçes*. In two respects in particular these great cathedrals with their far-reaching influence seem to have set a fashion which influenced all the after-Gothic of France and of the Continent in general. They both show a full development of the western façade with central *rosaçe* and sculptured portals below and flanked by towers. An earlier form of façade with more strongly marked horizontal lines is seen in such examples as Notre-Dame at Mantes and the Cathedral of Notre-Dame in Paris, but at Amiens and Reims it reached its perfection with predominant vertical lines and exquisite grace of adornment, and there is little wonder that the type of façade came to stay. In the matter of multiplication of aisles, with consequent elaboration of flying buttresses, the French Gothic plan also appears worked out to its perfection and henceforth in the typical Gothic church we have at the east end the wonderful grace and satisfying effect of a great polygonal apse with ambulatory and radiating chapels all connected together and spreading solidly to the ground by a forest of flying buttresses. This development of the *chevet* which Romanesque bequeathed to Gothic is one of the very happiest products of the growth of the latter on French soil.

Perhaps the most marvellous and beautiful of all

chevets of the kind is the Mid-Gothic example at Le Mans Cathedral, whose choir and transepts were built between 1215 and 1254. The internal effect of this choir with its double aisles, double clerestory and radiating chapels beyond is entrancing and appeals in an extraordinary way to the imagination.

A summary may here be given of churches which afford notable examples of early Gothic:

St.-Nicholas Blois, a Transitional church.

Notre-Dame Dijon, remarkable for its screen-front above the west porch or narthex. This is in two stages of very fine early pointed arcading, with three horizontal bands of elaborately carved foliage and grotesque figures, these last leaning in rows far out from the wall with curious effect.

Beaune (Côte-d'Or).

Candes (Indre-et-Loire), with beautiful south porch, whose vault is borne upon a slender central pillar.

Le-Puy-Nôtre-Dame (Maine-et-Loire).

St.-Nicholas Nantes—with good plate-tracery.

Meung (Loiret).

Ferrières (Loiret), a fine early west facade having a triplet of lancets and plain circle above.

Mussy-sur-Seine (Aube).

St.-Alpin Châlons-sur-Marne.

Mouzon (Ardennes) and Montierender (Haute-Marne), very splendid interiors on a large scale.

Hermonville (Marne).

Neufchâteau (Vosges).

Tannay (Nièvre).

St. Barnard Romans (Drôme).

St.-Yrieix (Hte.-Vienne).

St.-Léger Soissons.

St.-Leu-d'Esserent, St.-Jean-aux-Bois, Mello and Cires-lès-Mello (Oise). The first of these is an almost perfect example of unadorned Gothic, whose soaring movement is still held down by the Romanesque framework. It seems to blend in perfect measure Gothic lightness with Romanesque tenacity.

Ambrières (Mayenne).

Notre-Dame Verneuil-sur-Avre (Eure).

Clameçy (Nièvre).

St.-Pierre Bourges.

Vailly-sur-Aisne and Mont-Notre-Dame (Aisne).

(5) The Mid-Gothic and the Later or Flamboyant Type

While in their planning and general aspect the Gothic churches of France continued constant to type, details were developed or modified as time went on, so that we can distinguish phases of the style.

(A) The Mid-Gothic of the Fourteenth Century

Towards the end of the thirteenth century Gothic architecture passed into its middle phase, which lasted through the fourteenth century, when it lost some of the rigidity and severity it had inherited from its Romanesque ancestry and attained an ornate splendour through the development of geometrical tracery, the crocketing of pinnacles, spires and gables, a more lavish employment of statuary on the exterior and a multiplication of aisles, with a consequent elaboration of the system of flying buttresses. In this development the wonderful façades of Reims and Amiens led the way. There was no further development of plan or structural arrangement, but all that the later art of the fourteenth century could do was to add ornament, enlarge openings and lighten masses: and these things it did nobly and well.

The Mid-Gothic may be studied in very fine examples at:

The Cathedrals of Lyon, Nevers, Dijon, Auxerre, Soissons, Tours, Troyes; the choir and transepts of Le Mans and the façade of Sens.
St.-Pierre Chartres.[1]
Evron (Mayenne).
Puiseaux (Loiret).
St.-Satur (Cher).
St.-Jean-de-Vignes Soissons: a very beautiful fragment only, consisting of the cloister and the west façade of the church, with two unusually

---

[1] This very splendid church is remarkable for its excellent glass in the large clerestory windows and some beautiful panelling of Limoges enamel in the easternmost chapel.

graceful and ornate spires,[1] one of which is remarkable in having a crucifix worked in the tracery of its belfry-window.

Noyon Cathedral: the west end and towers.

St.-Germer (Oise): the eastern chapel added after the model of the Ste.-Chapelle in Paris.

Villeneuve-sur-Yonne (Yonne).

St.-Père-sous-Vézelay (Yonne). There is here an unusually fine west façade, with projecting porch of most beautiful design and a graceful and lofty tower at the north-west, at whose angles open arcading takes the place of buttresses as at Laon and Reims. The whole is an exquisite example of transition to Mid-Gothic (thirteenth century). Figures of trumpeting angels mask the angles at each receding stage of the tower, and these may be compared to the oxen in similar position on the west towers of Laon. Is it fanciful to suggest that these angels of St.-Père and the oxen of Laon might stand for the two chief factors in the unparalleled outburst of religious activity which raised these early Gothic churches—the visionary passion that aroused it as with a trumpet call from heaven, and the painful expenditure of labour, animal as well as human, that wrought the material embodiment of the vision?

Metz Cathedral: the vast height of the clerestory (the type of Bath Abbey, Sherborne Minster, Malvern Priory and St. Mary Redcliffe, but more fully carried out in earlier Gothic style) suggests the idea of a single-bodied structure whose mass is unbroken by a tower, the lateral accessory steeples being quite subordinate.

St.-Urbain Troyes: a church whose large and lofty clerestory windows, of geometrical tracery, render it a vast expanse of glass. In its general character it resembles the Cathedral of Metz.

St.-Julien Tours.

Varzy (Nièvre).

Dormans (Marne).

Chaumont (Hte.-Marne).

Augy (Aisne).

Mézières and Thugny (Ardennes).

Avioth (Meuse).

St. Maurice Épinal (Vosges).

La Chapelle-sous-Crécy and Rozoy (Seine-et-Marne).

(B) The Flamboyant of the Fifteenth Century

In the fifteenth century a further change came over the spirit of Gothic architecture. The plan of churches

[1] This façade, previously a ruin, was still further damaged in the Great War.

and the main lines of structure remained unaffected, but a double tendency made itself felt in design. Geometrical forms in tracery, in panelling and in parapets gave place more and more to flowing lines, until openings of wavy flame-like form entirely superseded the earlier geometrical patterns. From tracery of this kind the later French Gothic has earned the name Flamboyant. With this change in form there coincided a tendency to substitute open traceries for solid walls and fringes of tracery for arch-mouldings. In the result a typical church of this period appears as though draped with a veil of lace and the tracery of the richly decorated façades soars up in sprays of flame. The other tendency which belonged to later Gothic work was to work out the Gothic style to its logical conclusion and to emphasise its vertical tendency. The horizontal lines of the structure accordingly are subordinated and tend to disappear, the vertical lines of pier and vaulting shaft in the interior gaining additional prominence from the insignificance, or more commonly from the entire disappearance of the horizontal elements of abacus and capital.[1]

The following churches afford notable examples of the Flamboyant style:

Vendôme (Loir-et-Cher), a large towerless[2] church of great magnificence. Its west front shows typical tracery of the style, and a gable of open tracery is carried up above the great portal in a manner characteristic of the later Gothic.

La-Ferté-Bernard (Sarthe).

Notre-Dame-de-l'Épine (Marne).

Sens Cathedral—the transept ends.

Troyes Cathedral—the façade.

The churches of the Madeleine, St.-Nicholas, St.-Nizier, St.-Rémi and St.-Jean in Troyes.

---

[1] Details, with examples, are treated below, pp. 142, 143.

[2] A fine Romanesque tower with spire stands detached near the west end of the church.

St.-Michel Dijon.
St.-Nizier Lyon.
Ceffonds (Hte.-Marne).
Amagne and Rethel (Ardennes).
St.-Étienne Toul, a church of late Gothic showing a good deal of German influence in its design. But its west front is altogether of the French class and worthy to rank amongst the noblest of its kind.
St.-Nicholas-de-Port (Meurthe-et-Moselle).
Anet and the Chapelle-du-Champdé at Châteaudun (Eure-et-Loir).
Nantes Cathedral.
Orléans Cathedral, a finely proportioned example of belated Gothic of the reign of Henry IV.
Notre-Dame-la-Riche at Tours.
Senlis Cathedral—the transept ends.
St.-Pierre Senlis.
St.-Étienne Beauvais—the choir.
St.-Antoine and St.-Jacques Compiègne.

In the south are some good late Gothic churches at :

Mirepoix (Ariège).
The Cathedral of Aix-en-Provence.
Toulouse Cathedral.
St.-Michel and St.-Vincent Carcassonne.
St.-Just Narbonne (Aude).
St. Michel Bordeaux.
Montpellier Cathedral and Béziers, and Clermont-l'Hérault (Hérault).
Ste.-Radegonde Poitiers—the west front,

The north has some very splendid examples on a large scale, besides a large number of smaller churches. The following are particularly worthy of note :

St.-Wulfran Abbeville (Somme). A very lofty and magnificent nave with a façade like that of Amiens translated into terms of the Flamboyant style. In Ruskin's opinion this front well deserved for its exquisite beauty to be classed even with the great works of the thirteenth century.
St.-Ricquier (Somme), a large and spacious church with work of the finest detail. Its choir and transepts date from the fourteenth and its nave from the fifteenth century. The west façade of the sixteenth century is of the same general type as that of St.-Wulfran Abbeville, but it is designed with a large tower in the centre instead of the pair of towers typical of a French Gothic front. The portals are of the greatest beauty.

The Chapelle-St.-Esprit at Rue (Somme), a gem of lace-like work, lavishly adorned in the interior with statuary and carved work and having a screen of open tracery at the entrance to the inner chapel.

The churches of St.-Gilles, St.-Sépulcre and St.-Paul in Abbeville.

St.-Germain and St.-Leu Amiens.

Notre-Dame St.-Omer (Pas-de-Calais).

The ruined Abbey of St.-Bertin and the church of St.-Sépulcre at St.-Omer.

Aire-sur-La-Lys (Pas-de-Calais).

Ardres, Arques, and St.-Sauve Montreuil-sur-Mer (Pas-de-Calais).

Wismes (Pas-de-Calais), deserves mention for the beautiful panelling and sedilia in the apse.

St.-Maurice Lille.

Tourcoing, Roubaix, and St.-Eloi Dunkerque (Nord).

St.-Germain-l'Auxerrois and the Tour St.-Jacques in Paris.

In the north and north-east some late Gothic churches depart from the typical French *chevet* with its ambulatory and radiating chapels and follow the German or Flemish fashion in having an aisleless apse with very long windows as at the Dôm of Aix-la-Chapelle, the Cathedral of St.-Paul at Liège, the Abbey of Aulne and the churches of Hal, Huy and Tongres in Belgium. This arrangement is seen in France at Tourcoing and Roubaix (Nord), Hagenau (Bas-Rhin), Épinal (Vosges), Ceffonds (Hte.-Marne), St.-Urbain Troyes and St.-Michel Dijon.

(6) The Gothic Development in Normandy

During the period that followed upon the conquest of England this country and Normandy were linked together in a common development of architecture with an interchange of master-minds. Archbishop Lanfranc was engaged in building at Canterbury, Paul of Caen at St. Albans, and Gundulph, who came like Lanfranc from the Abbey of Bec, at Rochester, while on the other hand the priory of St.-Gabriel near Creully was founded by Robert of Gloucester in the earlier half of the twelfth century, and a century later the choir of Bayeux is attributed to the English bishop Henry

BEAUVAIS CATHEDRAL.

facing p. 112.

de Beaumont. Thus we find that in the great church-building era that ensued upon Duke William's Conquest of England, there was evolved on both sides of the Channel an Anglo-Norman type of Romanesque distinct from the round-arched style of other provinces or countries. Though some local variations may be traced yet in the later half of the eleventh century and in the earlier half of the twelfth, the style in Normandy and in England was in the main the same. Then came the innovation of the pointed arch, and Normandy, like the Ile-de-France, adopted it. But the early pointed architecture of Normandy is allied to that of England rather than to that of France. This was noted by Whewell long ago. "In the district west of Caen," he wrote, "almost every church has traces, more or less abundant, of Early English work; and these are generally very well characterised; and in their mouldings, bases, capitals, strings, buttresses, pinnacles, etc., remarkably faithful to the type existing in our own country." Every observant traveller will endorse this, for he cannot fail to notice the remarkably English look of the early-pointed churches about Caen and Bayeux, and conversely on returning to England he will be struck by the "Norman" appearance of such early stone spires as those of Oxford Cathedral and Witney (Oxon) or of village churches on and near the Sussex coast, like Pagham and Burpham. In Normandy, where almost every village church is full of interest, we come across the circular abacus that is so distinctive of Early English work, and that contrasts so strongly with the square abacus which the permanent influence of earlier Roman work preserved over the rest of France, not only in Romanesque buildings, but far on through the Gothic development. Again, in contrast to the apse so characteristic of French Gothic,

8

we meet, in Normandy, with very many examples of the rectangular east-end, and chancels of this plan have their doublet or triplet of lancets in the east wall, just like so many English parish churches of Sussex and of Kent.

The truth is that from the Conqueror's victory at Hastings the impulse of architecture, as of life in general, came from Normandy to England, and the record remains in the transept of Winchester, and the naves of Peterborough, Norwich, Gloucester and Tewkesbury: but from Henry's victory at Tinchebrai in 1106 the impulse and energy of the Anglo-Norman development was English. Thus Normandy took scarcely any part in the great architectural movement of transition, on the Continent, from Romanesque to Gothic, and it can show very few buildings of transitional style, though such may be met with near its borders. Normandy's first pointed style of architecture was Early English. Amongst the many village churches which exhibit this the following may be specially referred to in the department of Calvados:

Ryes, the choir with triplet of lancets at the east, and very pleasing doorway on the south side.

Demouville, Sacy, Branville and Pierrefitte all have the triple lancet in a square east end, in the last instance the three lights being included under a large containing arch.

Aizy has double lancets, and Frénouville and Quesnay have a double with circular window above in the east wall, a similar arrangement occurring in the west wall at Harcourt.

Cricqueville has three doublets of lancet-windows.

Typical Early English work also occurs at St.-Contest, Maltot, Hermanville, St.-Laurent-de-Condelles, Maisy, the Priory of Plessis-Grimoult and the west doorway at Rouvres.

Of the early Gothic in Normandy the noteworthy greater churches are as follows:

Bayeux Cathedral—the choir. This has, for its date, an unusually lofty triforium, and the pillars of the apse are coupled.

St.-Pierre Lisieux, a large cruciform church of Early English character with coupled shafts in the apse.

Coutances Cathedral—a very graceful and chaste example. Its apse has twin pillars like the two last-named churches. The inner aisle of the choir has a clerestory of its own, so that there is a double clerestory as at Beauvais, Bourges and Le Mans. This cathedral is also remarkable for the way in which the choir walls are strengthened at the spring of the apse. Flanking turrets with spires are set on either side of the clerestory, and these are connected by flying buttresses to similar turrets at the outer wall of the aisles. There is an arrangement of exactly the same kind in the early Gothic choir added to the Abbaye-aux-Hommes at Caen.

Rouen Cathedral is a grand and solemn example of early Gothic. The nave elevation is in four stories and the main triforium is open below the vaulting of the aisles. The triforium passage is oddly carried round on the capitals of the piers on the side towards the aisles, and is there corbelled out with clusters of detached pillars for support.

Gournay-en-Bray (Seine-Inférieure). In this case an early Gothic chancel and west front with lancet-windows has been added to a Romanesque nave. The east window is Mid-Gothic with good geometrical tracery in a square-ended chancel.

The Abbey of Fécamp and the church at Eu (Seine-Inférieure) are examples of plain early Gothic on a large scale, to which some later additions have been made.

St.-Sauveur Le Petit-Andelys (Eure).

After King John lost Normandy for the English Crown, the bond between the Province and England weakened, and each was more and more inclined to go its own way, Normandy naturally tending to become more French as time went on. We find accordingly that in churches of the Mid-Gothic and Flamboyant styles the fashion of building in Normandy was assimilated to the Gothic of France, and was no whit behind other parts of that country in raising the most splendid edifices.

Of Mid-Gothic churches in Normandy the best are :

Sées Cathedral—a building of much grace and charm. In the clerestory windows of the choir and apse are double planes of very beautiful tracery, of which the inner are glazed.

St.-Pierre Caen—a large church with much beautiful geometrical tracery.

St.-Ouen Rouen—the loveliest abbey church of France—of perfect "Decorated" work as it would be called in England. Its clerestory has the double planes of tracery which are a feature of Sées Cathedral.

Norrey (Calvados), which might be called the loveliest village church.

The Abbey of Ardennes (Calvados).

St.-Pierre-sur-Dives (Calvados). A large abbey church with portions of all dates from "Norman" Romanesque to late French Gothic.

Écouis (Eure). A church of small scale but of great charm on a cathedral or minster plan, with two west towers and central flèche.

Carentan (Manche), a church of very handsome exterior, of mixed Mid-Gothic and Flamboyant character.

Bricquebec (Manche).

Of the late French Gothic or Flamboyant style of the fifteenth and sixteenth centuries there are many examples :

In *Calvados* :

St.-Étienne-le-Vieux, St.-Gilles, St.-Jean, St.-Sauveur and St.-Ouen in Caen, besides the very ornate choir of St.-Pierre.

In Falaise the two churches of St.-Gervais and Ste.-Trinité.

St.-Léonard Honfleur, and the greater part of Vire.

In *Eure* :

This department has some of the best and most elaborately adorned examples of late Gothic in all France, such as :

The choir of Évreux Cathedral.

The towers of Rugles and the Madeleine Verneuil-sur-Avre.

St.-Ouen at Pont-Audemer.

The whole church of Ste.-Clotilde at Le Grand-Andelys.

The choir of Gisors and the porch of Louviers.

Other Flamboyant churches worthy of special notice are :

Notre-Dame and Ste.-Croix at Bernay, Conches, Pont-l'Évêque, Pont-de-l'Arche and Ivry-la-Bataille.

In *Orne* :

Argentan has the two large and splendid churches of St.-Germain and St.-Martin.

Mortagne and Alençon have important examples of the style, and beside should be noted the tower of St.-Martin at Laigle, the grand chancel of Exmes and Écouché and the church of Almenêches.

In *Manche* :

The finest late Gothic churches are at Valognes and Carentan, the latter remarkable for its beautiful tower and spire. The two churches of St.-Pierre and St.-Nicholas in Coutances are noteworthy. St.-L has some good work of the style, and there is much enriched deta at Ste.-Trinité Cherbourg.

In *Seine-Inférieure* :

On the grandest scale are the west façade and towers of Rouen Cathedra and the most beautiful octagonal lantern tower added (with sout transept front) to St.-Ouen in the same city.

St.-Maclou in Rouen is a well-known example, and by no means inferior to it is St.-Vincent in the same city. The towers of the desecrated church of St.-Laurent and of the vanished church of St.-André in Rouen also remain as evidences of the glories of the latest Gothic.

Caudebec-en-Caux has a complete church of the style which for extravagant adornment and beauty of design can scarcely be overpraised. Subordinate interior features such as *piscinæ* are of the most delicate design and execution. The apse has an even number of bays, so that the extreme east end is formed by an angle, and not by a flat side—a very unusual feature of planning. This wonderful church occupies amongst French parish churches a position analogous to that of St. Mary Redcliffe Bristol in England, for Henry IV, when he stayed at Caudebec, said that the town had "la plus jolie chapelle que j'ai jamais vu," while Queen Elizabeth named St. Mary Redcliffe as the fairest parish church in her realm.

In this Department also should be noted the churches of Harfleur, St.-Jacques and St.-Rémi in Dieppe, Arques-la-Bataille, St.-Jean and St.-Étienne Elbœuf, Longpaon, Cantileu, Le Tréport, the tower of Darnétal and the north-west porch at Montivilliers.

(7) The Architecture of Brittany

It is a fact, which has scarcely received the consideration it demands, that the Celtic districts of Western Europe present a curious agreement in their architectural history. In Brittany, Wales, Cumbria and Cornwall, examples of the Menhir and Dolmen are more numerous than in other parts of England or France. The stone ranks of Carnac, the circles of Stonehenge, and the cromlechs of Finistère, Pembrokeshire and Cornwall are alike famous, and equally without influence on the architecture of later times. When we come to Christian architecture we find that other Celtic districts agree with Brittany in that their structures, generally speaking, are quite early or very late. Cornwall has some remains of small rectangular oratories of early Christianity,[1] and a little Norman work. Village churches in Wales often preserve in their form, and absence of detail,

[1] Interesting examples remain in St. Pirran's oratory at Perranzabuloe, and the chapel at St. Madron's Well near Penzance.

the appearance of early sanctuaries. Both districts agree in a general absence of work of the great Gothic development, and an overwhelming predominance of late Perpendicular of the close of the fifteenth and early part of the sixteenth centuries.[1] Similarly Brittany shows few churches earlier than the fourteenth century. Its internal condition of confusion and anarchy prevented any architectural development during the great constructive period, just as Wales was distracted by internal factions and desolated by the wars of Owain Glyndwr. The case of Brittany is therefore somewhat parallel to that of Wales, and its distinctive local style is of the latest Flamboyant Gothic belonging to the end of the fifteenth and to the sixteenth centuries. The case of Brittany, however, is unlike that of Wales in having with its late Gothic an admixture of Renaissance, for in Brittany no religious change, corresponding to the Reformation in England and Wales, intervened to check church building.[2] It is this creeping in of classical feeling, or engrafting of classical detail, upon a general design of late Gothic, of somewhat heavy character owing to the local material of granite, that gives to Breton architecture its peculiar and characteristic expression, such as finds no exact parallel elsewhere.

Early work in Brittany does not call for much remark. St.-Gildas-de-Rhuys (Morbihan) has a venerable Romanesque choir and apse of a church which is said to go back to the eleventh century, and there is a fine church

[1] The case of Galicia in Spain is strangely parallel. The early Romanesque is found at Santiago de Compostella in juxtaposition with a very florid type of late Renaissance, and the metropolitical church is, in its architecture, typical of the Province. There is in Galicia no existing example of a finished Gothic church, and no example even of transition from Romanesque to Gothic.

[2] There is scarcely any Renaissance work in Wales, but a not ungraceful spirelet was added in the style to the church at Llangoedmore (Cardigan), and in domestic work there is a very fine gateway at Beaupré (Glamorgan).

later in the style (1180–90) at Loctudy (Finistère). At Lanleff (Côtes-du-Nord) is a ruined circular church of the Holy Sepulchre of the twelfth century. This is of a severe type of Romanesque with square piers, the rude carving of the capitals of shafts attached to these forming the only adornment. There was another round church, assigned to the eleventh century, at Quimperlé (Finistère), of which the present Ste.-Croix is a nineteenth-century reconstruction. Besides some complete churches, such as those just mentioned, we meet with a Romanesque portion of a church here and there. Amongst these fragments preserved when churches were rebuilt or altered at a later time, there are deserving of special mention the south porch of Notre-Dame-de-la-Clarté at Perros-Guirec (Côtes-du-Nord), the more elaborate portal with a range of three arches at St.-Sauveur Dinan (Côtes-du-Nord) and the tower of St.-Sauveur Redon (Ille-et-Vilaine). At Daoulas (Finistère) are preserved the arcades of what must have been a very fine cloister belonging to the twelfth century.

About the Romanesque of this part of France there is, however, nothing distinctive of the locality. It was in the late Gothic period that Breton architects developed their own peculiar style, exhibiting curious features, amongst which the following are notable:

(A) The local type of parapet is of open work with many vertical lines placed close together, as seen in the towers at Quimper Cathedral, Pleyben, Lambader, Le Folgoët, St.-Michel Quimperlé and Ploaré (Finistère) and Carnac (Morbihan).

(B) There is a good deal of rather elaborate geometrical tracery either in windows or in blind panelling, as at Quimper Cathedral, Tréguier Cathedral, the Cathedral and the Kreisker church at St.-Pol-de-Léon (Finistère) and some wonderfully well-designed examples at the fountain of the Carmelites at Morlaix (Finistère) and the porch of Pont-Croix (Finistère), which in addition to the elaborate panelling of its lofty gable and side-buttresses has also pierced geometrical tracery in the head of the entrance arch.

LA-ROCHE-MAURICE (FINISTÈRE).

(C) The exigencies of the unsettled and troubled condition of the district produced in Brittany a remarkable local variety of tower design, particularly characteristic of the department of Finistère. In this pagoda-like type of tower, stage is superimposed upon stage, each one being crowned by a gallery running round all four sides. The district was, in the Middle Ages, continually exposed to the ravages of French and English alike, and tower design was modified that the structure might serve for a watch-tower or look-out, whence the approach of a hostile force or of a plundering band of raiders might be observed at a distance, and due warning be given to the inhabitants. The peculiar form of tower survived even when the actual need for the watching galleries passed away—for architecture everywhere has always been very conservative of forms—hence the characteristic tower of western Brittany, with galleries in receding stages, is found alike in late Gothic and in the Renaissance towers by a local school of architects belonging to the later half of the sixteenth century and the earlier half of the seventeenth. These towers occur at:

Gouesnou, Huelgoat, La-Roche-Maurice, Pencran, Locquirec, and Loctudy (Finistère) and Brélévenez (Côtes-du-Nord), while good later Renaissance examples are at the church of Croaz—Baz Roscoff (Finistère) and Ploubezre (Côtes-du-Nord).

(D) A characteristic variant of the towers just mentioned is an oblong belfry consisting of a sort of screen-gallery. This generally has a tall crocketed spirelet in the centre, containing the bells, flanked by smaller spirelets or pinnacles at the ends of the gallery. Well-designed instances of this peculiarly Breton belfry are found at Guimiliau, Le Faoüet, Plougastel and Penmarch (Finistère) and the Chapelle-de-St.-Quay at Perros-Guirec (Côtes-du-Nord)—the last a Renaissance example. A single spirelet of late Gothic design is not uncommon for a belfry, as at Pont-Aven (Finistère).

(E) A lateral porch is much more common than in France generally, and is, in fact, quite usual as a feature of a Breton church.

(F) Owing to the distinctive Breton blend of late Gothic design with classical detail, pinnacles and finials frequently take a very odd form, resembling rather fantastically shaped chess-men, as seen especially in the churches of Finistère—Sizun, Lampaul-Guimiliau, Ploaré, La-Roche-Maurice, and, in the greatest profusion, at St.-Thégonnec.

It was of course only natural that the French Gothic or the early Gothic of Normandy should make occasional inroads into Brittany, and fine examples of "French" churches occur, as at St.-Sauveur Dinan, St.-Brieuc, Tréguier (Côtes-du-Nord), Vitré (Ille-et-Vilaine), Quimper and St.-Pol-de-Léon Cathedrals, and the Kreisker church at St.-Pol-de-Léon (Finistère) and Vannes Cathedral (Morbihan). At Dol is an excellent example of early Gothic of the Normandy type.

In concluding this part of our subject something must be said with reference to the very striking adjuncts of Breton churches, which are specially characteristic of this part of France.

The sacred enclosure of the churchyard is frequently entered through an imposing *Triumphal Arch*. There is a good one of simple design at Lampaul, and more elaborate ones, of typical Breton style, with ranges of three openings at St.-Thégonnec (sixteenth century) and Argol (seventeenth century), while at Sizun is a very grand example of good seventeenth-century classical design surmounted by an open balustrated parapet, and bearing aloft the three crosses of Calvary above its central archway.

On passing through the arch one finds that the parish church forms the centre-piece of a striking group of structures, embracing an ossuary, calvary and in many cases also a sacred well. Altogether the most impressive and characteristic group of the kind is the one at St.-Thégonnec (Finistère).

The *Calvaries* are specially interesting owing to the peculiar local treatment which monuments of this kind received. From very early times the Bretons, with Christians in general, were wont to erect the sacred sign of the Cross or Crucifix by the wayside and in public places, and in this respect we find another similarity between Brittany and Cornwall, the Calvaries of Brittany finding a parallel in the almost innumerable wayside and churchyard crosses of the English county, though their design and execution differ greatly, the Cornish examples being for the most part the rudely executed wheel-crosses of an early date. As Christianity spread throughout Europe sites consecrated to an earlier worship were adapted for Christian sacred uses, and in Brittany the early missionaries of the Faith converted dolmens into chapels and erected crosses upon menhirs. Several instances are still extant and one of the most remarkable is the Menhir of Champ-Dolent near Dol (Ille-et-Vilaine). This monument is a monolith thirty feet high, formerly surmounted by a stone Calvary which was destroyed at the Revolution, and has since been replaced by a crucifix of wood. The menhirs of St.-Duzec (Côtes-du-Nord) and Pensarn (Finistère) received a different treatment and bear engraved upon their surfaces a full series of the recognised emblems of the Passion with the figure of Christ crucified. A monolith at Lan-ar-Justiz (Côtes-du-Nord) has been likewise Christianised by having attached to it by iron clamps a crucifix with its attendant figures; of these the statue of Our Lady remains alone. Near Trégastel (Côtes-du-Nord) is a crucifix of primitive type with figure sculpture in low relief upon its base, and there is another early example at St.-Avé (Morbihan). Calvaries of comparatively simple form also occur at Ploubezre (Côtes-du-Nord), Lampaul-Guimiliau, St.-Jean-Trolimen, St.-Thégonnec, Commana, Pencran and Plovan (Finistère) and Melrand (Morbihan), the last having at its head a conventional representation of the Holy Trinity. At Ploubezre (Côtes-du-Nord) is a curious row of five crosses in line, upon the centre and tallest of which is the figure of Christ.

But in the sixteenth and seventeenth centuries an extraordinary and unique development in Calvary design took place in the hands of a local school of artists whose work is seen in the examples at Plougastel, Guimiliau, Pleyben, Plougonven, Comfort, Quililen, St.-Thégonnec and Tronoan (all in Finistère). In these the Crucifix with attendant figures—at Plougastel, Pleyben, St.-Thégonnec and Tronoan the three crosses of Calvary—rise high above a large square base, upon which, as on a platform, groups of figures are set, portraying the drama of the Passion and a whole Theology of the Atonement. The sides of the spreading base below are further adorned with sculpture in high relief depicting scenes related to the Passion.

An accessory to the church characteristic of Breton ecclesiology which sometimes attains great size and architectural splendour is the *Ossuaire*, where bones of the deceased parishioners are stored that the burying-space within the consecrated churchyard may be used over again. The *ossuaire* is sometimes a small annexe at the side of a church porch, like the domed rotunda at Trégastel (Côtes-du-Nord), or the structure of dainty Renaissance design at St.-Herbot (Finistère). But the characteristic Breton ossuary is a detached building varying in size from the little arcaded example at St.-Pol-de-Léon (Finistère) to the splendid ones at Pencran, Pleyben, St.-Thégonnec and Sizun. These are as large and ornate as many a village church, with traceried windows at Pleyben and St.-Thégonnec and fine external arcading at Pencran and Sizun, with in the last-named some beautiful statuary in niches. A structure related to these last in its uses, and which may, therefore, be grouped with them, is the sepulchral chapel at St.-Jean-du-Doigt (Finistère), a square building in the churchyard, with tiled roof and open sides, supported on massive columns of late classical pattern resembling table-legs. Altogether this chapel forms the greatest possible contrast to the beautiful and delicate Chapelle-des-Morts at Avioth (Meuse).[1]

Holy Wells abound in Brittany as in the Celtic districts

[1] See below, p. 206.

of Cornwall and Wales in Britain. These are usually canopied over, sometimes with rudely-piled stones as at Ste.-Marie-du-Menez-Horn (Finistère), but more often with gracefully worked gables of late Gothic style, as at Le Folgoët, St.-Vennec (Finistère), Baud and St.-Nicodème (Morbihan). The well at Carnac has a *baldachino* of heavy classical design, while those of St.-Jean-du-Doigt (Finistère) and Loguivy (Côtes-du-Nord) are circular fountains with graceful and slender centre-pieces of the seventeenth century.

(8) The Arrangement of Towers

Before passing on to consider the principal details of French Gothic style, it may be well to conclude this chapter upon its planning and general character by some notice of the disposition and arrangement of towers in the churches of France.

Speaking quite generally we may say that French church towers from the Romanesque style onwards were in most churches central or lateral, the central tower being a translation into Romanesque of the cupola or lantern round which grouped the centralised plan of a Byzantine church and the lateral tower on the other hand tracing back to the Italian campanile, in its origin a structure detached from the church. The central-towered plan is common and characteristic of the churches over a large part of France—in Burgundy, towards the east, in Périgord, Saintonge and Poitou in the west and in Normandy towards the north.

Axial Towers

The Abbey church of St.-Martin d'Ainay at Lyon seems to be the earliest example in France of the axial arrangement of towers. In addition to the low central tower at the crossing, another taller square tower rises in the centre of the west façade. A like arrangement occurs again, as we go up the Rhône valley, at Cruas (Ardèche) and at Champdieu (Loire). This disposition of towers is the usual one in the peculiar local Romanesque of Auvergne, as seen in the large and important churches of Notre-Dame-du-Port Clermont-Ferrand, Issoire (Puy-de-Dôme) and Brioude (Hte.-Loire). Axial towers also are found at St.-Junien (Hte.-Vienne), Bénévent-l'Abbaye and Chambon-sur-Vouèze (Creuse), St.-Aventin (Hte.-Garonne), St.-Désiré (Allier), St.-Aignan-sur-Cher (Loir-et-Cher), Neuil-sur-l'Autize and Maillezais (Vendée), Poissy (Seine-et-Oise) and Loches (Indre-et-Loire). Externally the effect of axial towers is given to the fine churches of Le Dorat (Hte.-Vienne) and St.-Benoît-sur-Loire (Loiret) by the grouping of a central tower with the lofty mass of a sort of narthex tower at the west end. All these churches referred to are Romanesque. The like planning is found in a late Gothic church at St.-Jean in Caen and at St.-Pierre Coutances. The two towers of the last-named classicalise in their detail, as also does the unfinished central tower of St.-Jean Caen, but they are well conceived and group splendidly with the octagonal lantern and western spires of the cathedral close by. The placing of the towers on the main axis of a building gives a very satisfactory outline to the external elevation, and from no point of view do the towers become confused. Most of the examples of this planning are, however, Romanesque in style, and it did not become a favourite arrangement with the Gothic builders.[1]

[1] In England also the plan was rarely adopted, Ely Cathedral and Wimborne Minster, besides the partly ruined church at Wymondham (Norfolk), being the only churches which now exhibit it on a large scale, but Hereford Cathedral, Malmesbury and Shrewsbury Abbeys and Christchurch Priory (Hants) used to have it. There are axial towers to the parish churches at Purton (Wilts), Old Clee (Lincs) and Horfield near Bristol.

Group of Three Towers—one Central and Two Western

Quite early in the Romanesque style the central tower was set off by building two other towers at the west end, forming a group of three in which the western pair were originally intended to be subsidiary to the dominant central feature of the whole church.

In Burgundy we have the three-towered plan on a large scale at Tournus and Paray-le-Monial (Saône-et-Loire), though at Tournus the south-west tower remains in what is apparently its original condition, with gabled finish, and has never been carried up to match its fellow-tower of the façade. The Cathedral of Autun is another example with two Romanesque west towers, but in this case the central tower has received a late Gothic upper stage, with crocketed spire. Semur-en-Auxois (Côte-d'Or) shows a three-towered outline complete, its central octagon Romanesque, with two western towers flanking the typical Burgundian narthex-porch and completed in late Gothic. Auxonne (Côte-d'Or) was also designed for three towers, but only one of the western pair rises to its full height.

Of the Romanesque churches of Auvergne St.-Nectaire (Puy-de-Dôme) and Mauriac (Cantal) are somewhat exceptional in having a group of three towers, both these churches having twin towers at the west end in place of the single tower more usual in that position in the district. At Conques (Aveyron) is another fine Romanesque church of the *Massif Central* with three well-proportioned towers.

In the Norman Romanesque we have an early example of a three-towered church at the Abbey of Jumièges (Seine-Inférieure). Then, a little later, followed other instances of the like plan at the "Norman" churches of St.-Georges-de-Boscherville (Seine-Inférieure) and the two great Abbeys at Caen. Bayeux Cathedral and the early Gothic Cathedral of Coutances came next with St.-Pierre Lisieux, and St.-Pierre-sur-Dives (Calvados). The "Early English" looking church of Dol (Ille-et-Vilaine) is of the same plan as regards its towers, and such arrangement is found in early Gothic as far to the south as the fine example at St.-Nicholas at Blois. In the later Gothic we find it at Rouen Cathedral, St.-Ouen in Rouen and Le Grand-Andelys (Eure). The Cathedral of Évreux has three towers, but the pair at the west end are of the Renaissance style, and Gisors (Eure) was planned for three towers, only one of which, standing at the north of the west front, is completed, in very fine Renaissance design.

In some of these three-towered churches the grouping of the towers is very striking, owing to the fact that the two western towers are quite unlike in design. This is the case at the Cathedrals of Rouen and Évreux, at St.-Pierre-sur-Dives and St.-Pierre Lisieux. To the highly picturesque and diversified outline presented by such churches as these English church architecture now affords no parallel.[1] When the three-towered plan is adopted the two western towers usually stand at the end of the aisles, but occasionally, as at Rouen Cathedral, the towers flanking the west front stand out beyond the aisles to the north and south.[2] This disposition gives a magnificent breadth of frontage at the west, so that the façade of Rouen is amongst the most imposing of Cathedral fronts. Yet the wide spacing of towers

[1] In English churches with three towers the west towers are uniform. But at Canterbury previous to 1840 a "Norman" tower stood at the north-west angle, and gave to the cathedral a varied outline, unique for an English church, since destroyed by the assimilation of the western towers.

[2] Wells Cathedral affords a parallel in England.

Photo by G. T. Parratt

CHARTRES CATHEDRAL FROM N.W.

Photo by G. T. Parratt.

CHARTRES CATHEDRAL, W. PORTAL.

EARLY GOTHIC.

facing p. 128.

involved is not altogether satisfactory, for the western towers do not group so well with the central one in a general view as when they are set at the ends of the aisles and are therefore closer together.

The beautiful plan of a group of three towers is thus widely distributed and was especially adopted by the Anglo-Norman builders for their greater churches on both sides of the Channel. Thus we have the three-towered outline at Southwell Minster and Durham Cathedral of "Norman" churches, and it became the typical English Gothic Cathedral plan, as seen at Canterbury, Chichester, Wells, Lichfield, Lincoln, York and Ripon.

In France the beautiful Romanesque church of Morienval (Oise) is also a three-towered church, but of different planning. The single tower in this case is at the west end and groups effectively with twin towers of smaller dimensions that flank the spring of the apse.

Transeptal Towers

The towers are occasionally set north and south of the centre of the church, so that they rise from a bay of the transept. But the external effect of such grouping can scarcely be judged fairly, because in so very few cases have both towers been completed. At St.-Stephen's Vienna only one of the towers has received its tapering spire. The Cathedrals of Angoulême and Le Mans have not been more fortunate, for in both cases only one of the intended pair has been built—at Angoulême, the one rising from the outer bay of the north transept and at Le Mans the one in the corresponding position on the south. Murbach in Alsace has its Romanesque twin transeptal towers placed close together so as almost to form one central feature and there is a charming Mid-Gothic example of like design at Varzy (Nièvre).

9

St.-Salvi at Albi has its towers set at the transept ends but projecting westwards beyond the transept walls. The great Abbey of St.-Martin at Tours, destroyed at the Revolution, should apparently be added to the list of churches with transeptal towers, one of these towers still remaining forlorn. This arrangement of towers is found alike in some Gothic and Romanesque churches and in places very far apart, such as San Abbondio Como in Italy, the Cathedrals of Geneva and Barcelona and Cormac's Chapel on the rock of Cashel in Ireland, but it never seems to have found much favour. The only English cathedral that has transeptal towers is Exeter and at Ottery St. Mary in Devon the same arrangement was adopted from the Cathedral Church.

There are two cases where a great church appears in a general view as though it had transeptal towers, but a closer inspection discloses a different planning. The pair of lateral towers at the unfinished late Gothic church of St.-Just Narbonne were designed to flank the choir to the east of a transept which has not been built. Again, at the Cathedral of Metz there are two lateral steeples. In this case they are markedly oblong in plan, and rising above porches on the north and south, about midway along the length of the nave they seem to be striving to look at one another over its vast body. The tower on the south has been completed with a spirelet flanked by slender pinnacles with flying buttresses.

Group of Four Towers

A four-towered design found some favour in Germany. Halle shows four slender towers, two at the west end with tapering spires and the eastern pair flanking the choir having domical finish. Andernach in Rhenish Prussia also shows a group of four towers, and we meet with a like arrangement at Arnstein, although in this last case the church is not cruciform. Other examples in Germany of more graceful outline occur at the Cathedrals of Bamberg and Naumberg. These churches both have the German characteristic western apse in addition to the usual apse at the east end, and a pair of towers flanks the apse at either end. In France Lyon Cathedral is an example of a four-towered church. Two towers here flank the façade at the west end in the usual French fashion, while the other two are transeptal, being set outside the aisles and forming a genuine transept to the church. The church of the Madeleine at Vézelay now shows three towers of an intended group of four. Two of these are in the regular position at the west front and the third stands in the angle between the nave and south transept, rising above the south aisle and evidently intended to be matched by a corresponding tower to the west of the north transept. The Abbey of St.-Martin at Laon has an exactly parallel arrangement of its four dominant features, but the two flanking the façade are scarcely more than turrets in their proportion. Notre-Dame at Châlons-sur-Marne must be reckoned amongst four-towered churches, for in addition to the pair of Romanesque towers which flank the choir, as at the Cathedral in the same city, Notre-Dame has also two very fine early Gothic towers crowned by leaded spires flanking the west façade. An early Gothic example at St.-Leu-d'Esserent (Oise) has in addition to its two western towers a pair with gabled finish set one on either side at the spring of the apse. It is very probable that the Abbey of Tours already referred to ought to be reckoned also amongst French churches of four-towered design. The two remaining towers stand on either side of the modern street which runs where the great nave of the church formerly stood. From the position of

these two towers in relation to the church as shown in ar
old print reproduced in the Abbé Chevalier's "Promen
ades Pittoresques en Touraine," it would appear that th
tower now known as the "Tour de l'Horloge" wa
the southern tower of a pair at the west end, while th

NOTRE-DAME CHÂLONS-SUR-MARNE (MARNE).

so-called "Tour Charlemagne" stood at the nort
transept.

It cannot be claimed that the grouping of four towe
is artistic in its effect. There is about it a want
decision and of striking outline, and this is especially tl
case when, as at the Cathedral of Lyon, the towers ri
but little above the roof of the church.

Multiple Groups of Seven or Nine Towers

A much more intricate external effect was arrived at by the builders of the Cathedrals of Laon and Rouen. In each of these cases a majestic group of seven towers was contemplated. At Rouen three of these, the central tower with its modern spire of open ironwork and the two western towers, the Tour de Beurre with its rich octagon and the Tour St. Romain with its lofty hipped roof, soar to a great height, and are most picturesque in their variety. The remaining four towers flank the transept façades on the north and south and are very beautifully designed with long openings, but they were never completed and do not rise above the transept roof, so that the intended effect has not been attained, and we cannot at Rouen judge of the appearance of a seven-towered church. Though seven-towered on the plan, it is, in a general exterior view, a three-towered church. Laon Cathedral has scarcely been more fortunate. The arrangement of the towers is the same as at Rouen, viz., a central tower at the crossing, two at the west front, and a pair flanking each transept to north and south, making seven in all, but few of them are finished. The designing is good and the appearance of the towers unusually light owing to the open arcading of the angle turrets. The towers at the west façade are carried up to a considerable height and form a graceful pair, but the central tower rises only a little above the crossing, while of the transept towers only the ones at the north-west and south-west angles show themselves as towers, the remaining two not rising to the level of the roof. The result is a confused grouping of dominant features which is far from satisfactory in a general view. With Laon and Rouen should be classed the Cathedral of Clermont-Ferrand, designed to bear a similar sevenfold crown of towers. Until recently, however, only one tower was carried up above the roof-line—the one set at the eastern angle of the north transept façade. It was reserved for the architect Viollet-le-Duc to complete the western twin spires, which he wisely built in the native black volcanic stone, so that now Notre-Dame de Clermont presides, in its dark and somewhat sinister beauty, over the city, clustering upon the hill-sides, with the usual French dominant feature of twin western towers.[1]

More wonderful still would have been the exteriors of the Cathedrals of Chartres and Reims if the purposes of the architects had been fully carried out, for these were intended to have a cluster of eight towers around a ninth and central one, the arrangement being as at Laon and Rouen, but with the addition of a pair of towers flanking the great apse. At Chartres, however, there is on an outside view no sign of the central tower and the six towers intended to flank the transept fronts and the apse have not been carried up above the level of the clerestory, so that only the two at the west end have been finished, and these at dates widely apart and in very different styles. Reims Cathedral, too, is equally an example of unfulfilled aspirations, for there only the western towers rise above the level of the roof, and even these are unfinished, ending abruptly and in a makeshift fashion, without the tall traceried spires which one cannot but imagine they must have been designed to bear.

[1] At Limburg-am-Lahn in Germany alone do we see a seven-towered plan carried to completion. There the central octagon with its spire rises well above the surrounding towers, giving unity to the whole conception. The style is the somewhat heavy native German Romanesque and the general effect is scarcely satisfactory, for the towers at the transept ends are little more than turrets, and owing to the shortness of the nave and transepts the towers seem huddled together, and the building appears cramped by the towers.

Two Towers at the West Façade only

The Cathedrals of Chartres and Reims just alluded to illustrate in a remarkable manner how the fondness of French architects for soaring vaults to their churches resulted in the abandonment of all towers except the pair at the west end, and the excessive height to which it became the fashion to raise the vault is sometimes not without its detrimental effect even upon the western towers, which remained a constant feature. The pair at St.-Wulfran Abbeville, for example, scarcely rise above the ridge of the great nave behind them, and those of Amiens Cathedral are more seriously interfered with—in fact they can scarcely be called towers. The one to the south is lower than the ridge of the nave roof, and both are squeezed into oblong form, so that they are little more than a sort of screen finish to the wonderful façade to which the appearance of a pair of towers has been given on the western face. The disappearance of the central tower, and of towers at the transept ends, is thus characteristic of French Gothic in its full development, and a grand west front with deeply recessed portals and crowned by a pair of towers became the regular design.

Sometimes the two towers at the west façade are really twin towers—identical in design—as at:

Notre-Dame Paris.
Reims Cathedral.
Mantes (Seine-et-Oise).
St.-Wulfran Abbeville (Somme).
Nantes Cathedral.
Quimper Cathedral.
Orléans Cathedral.
Mézières (Ardennes).
Chaumont (Hte.-Marne).
Avioth (Meuse).
St.-Léon Nancy.
Montpellier Cathedral.
La-Chaise-Dieu (Hte.-Loire).
St.-Maurice Vienne (Isère).
Bayonne Cathedral.
Sées Cathedral.
St.-Étienne Toul (Meurthe-et-Moselle).
Pont-à-Mousson (Meurthe-et-Moselle).
St.-Nicholas-de-Port (Meurthe-et-Moselle).
Dijon Cathedral.
The Carmelite church Le Puy.
Écouis (Eure).
Notre-Dame-du-Marthuret Riom (Puy-de-Dôme).

In very many cases, however, the two towers of the west front are more or less dissimilar, as in the churches of:

Poitiers Cathedral.
Noyon Cathedral.
St.-Jean-de-Vignes Soissons.
Souvigny (Allier).
Notre-Dame-de l'Épine (Marne).
Rodez Cathedral.
Mende Cathedral.
Amiens Cathedral.
St.-Lô (Manche).
St.-Brieuc (Côtes-du-Nord).
Bourges Cathedral.
St.-Nizier Lyon.
St.-Flour (Cantal).
Tours Cathedral.

At Chartres and Senlis the steeples of the façade are so far removed in date and design as to be altogether unlike, with curious effect in a general view.

There are cases also where only one of an intended pair at the west front has been erected, as at Auxerre, Sens, Meaux and Troyes Cathedrals.

That the arrangement of two towers at the west end is the characteristic one in the developed mediæval architecture of France is further seen from the fact that in the Renaissance style we find it still adhered to for cathedrals and the more important churches, such as the following:

Auch Cathedral.
Rennes Cathedral.
Langres Cathedral.
Verdun Cathedral.
St.-Christophe, Belfort (Haut-Rhin).
St.-Michel Dijon.
St.-Sulpice Paris.
Corbie (Somme).
Vitry-le-François (Marne).

Reference should here be made to the peculiar treatment which the west front of the cathedral at Angers has received. The upper stages of the two towers seem to be a late imitation of Romanesque and are crowned by Gothic crocketed spires, but they were once finished with wooden spires, and were, like some German towers,[1] joined by a bridge. Early in the sixteenth

[1] Two towers are connected by a bridge, or flying gallery, at some height above the roof of a church at the Magdalenenkirche Breslau, at Halle and at Dietkirchen.

century spires and bridge were rebuilt in stone, but a fire in 1531 resulted in a rebuilding of the northern tower in a richer form, and a third tower arose between the pair. This is of the same kind of pseudo-Romanesque as the upper part of the towers, and is crowned by a cupola belonging more distinctly to the Renaissance. The giving of extra height to a façade by the interposition of a structure between the western towers only finds a parallel in France at Le Neubourg (Eure), but was not uncommon in Germany, being the local fashion at Brunswick, as seen at the Cathedral and St.-Catherine's, and occurring elsewhere, as at Meissen on the Elbe in Saxony.

Tréguier Cathedral is unique in France in having three towers in line in the centre of the building. There is a low tower at the crossing, an earlier Romanesque tower at the south transept, and another with late Gothic wind-holed spire, rises from the north transept end.

At St.-Jean Dijon a pair of towers is curiously set at the east end. These towers must have been originally erected in the angles between the choir and transepts; but a curtailment of the chancel when the present roadway was made has brought them into the position of twin towers of an eastern façade. Reference should here also be made to the strange effect produced by the unusual arrangement at Valognes (Manche), where a lofty bell-tower stands in the angle between the north transept and the choir close to the central octagonal lantern with a pointed dome. The pierced parapet of the octagon very oddly skips across the narrow intervening space and encircles the tower below the belfry stage. Both towers are of very late Gothic, with a tendency to classicalism, but their grouping is striking and effective.

One Tower at the West End

The single western tower—usual and characteristic in English parochial churches—is not a prevailing feature

Valognes (Manche).

in French church architecture, but is not uncommon in two localities especially. We find it in Normandy, where the architecture naturally has affinities with England in such churches as Bernières-sur-Mer, Colleville-sur-Mer, Villers-sur-Mer and St.-Jacques Lisieux (Calvados), but even here where the tower is not central it is more often lateral than at the west end. Again, in the north there are many examples of churches with one tower at the west end. The prevalence of the western tower in the churches of Pas-de-Calais gives them an English look. Thus, the churches of St.-Omer, Notre-Dame, St.-Denis, St.-Sépulcre and the Abbey of St.-Bertin, all have a great tower at the west end of the nave, and we find the same feature on a splendid scale at Aire-sur-la-Lys, St.-Waast Béthune (Pas-de-Calais), St. Ricquier (Somme), St.-Maurice Lille and St.-Pierre Douai (Nord). It was usual too in many a village church, such as those of Loos and Souchez, which perished in the Great War. The preference for one large tower at the west end as the dominant feature in the elevation of a church runs throughout Flanders, as is witnessed by the majority of churches on both sides of the Franco-Belgian border, and by the examples on a large scale of Malines Cathedral, the Cathedrals of Bruges and Ghent, and important churches such as St.-Jacques Antwerp and St.-Martin at Ypres.

Detached Towers

The earliest towers were not designed as part of the church to which they belonged, but were separate structures intended to hold the bells, and were either wholly detached or only connected with the main building by some subsidiary part. To this type of tower the church builders of North Italy remained faithful, and accordingly the typical and best-known Italian towers are detached campaniles as at the Cathedrals of Pisa, Florence, Cremona and St. Mark's Venice. In the architecture of northern Europe, on the other hand, the tower is regularly designed as part of the structure of the church and we meet with occasional examples only of detached towers. Romanesque examples occur in France at St.-Germain Auxerre, Brantôme, Ste.-Trinité Vendôme and the Cathedral of Le Puy. The city of Bordeaux has two fine late Gothic examples; the cathedral bell-tower known as La-tour-Pey-Berland, and the very tall hexagonal tower and spire standing on open arches at a little distance from the façade of St.-Michel.[1] St.-Émilion (Gironde) has a tall tower with crocketed spire above its curious rock church, and there is another detached tower at Viviers. St.-Martin Étampes (Seine-et-Oise) has a massive tower, which leans very much from the perpendicular, near its west end, and other good Gothic detached towers occur at Darnétal near Rouen, St.-Sauveur Redon (Ille-et-Vilaine) and St.-Éloi Dunkerque (Nord). There is a very plain Renaissance example at St.-Sever (Calvados). Ste.-Catherine Honfleur (Calvados)—itself constructed in wood—is unique in France in having a detached wooden belfry standing, an extremely picturesque object, in the midst of the market-place over against the church's western front.

[1] In some instances a western tower stands on open arches, as at Villefranche-de-Rouergue (Aveyron), Blangy (Calvados), Sainte-Solange (Cher) and some churches in the Pyrénées such as St. Jean-de-Luz, Hendaye and Oloron-Ste.-Marie. Occasionally another part of a church is built over a right of way, and therefore has an arched passage beneath it. This gives a very picturesque external effect to the east ends of St.-Pierre on Mont-St.-Michel, Ste.-Trinité Falaise (Calvados) and Triel (Seine-et-Oise). At Dannes (Pas-de-Calais) the late fifteenth-century choir bestrides a little river and the sacristy is built in a bay over the waterway.

CHAPTER VI

GOTHIC—ITS DETAILS

HAVING dealt, in the last chapter, with the origin and development of Gothic architecture in France, its planning and general features, and its notable local phases, it will now be necessary to give some account of its characteristic detail of design.

(1) PILLARS, ARCHES AND CAPITALS

With regard to the pillars, their capitals and the arches sustained by them, no one can help being impressed by the very conservative character of French Gothic. In the early Gothic, the cylindrical pillar and Corinthianesque capital were retained, so that the arcade often has a classical look such as we do not find in the "Early English" of Normandy and England. This classical flavour lingered about the pillars of French churches all through the Gothic development and was still further emphasised by the retention of the square abacus, which was deserted in England for an abacus of rounded form. The long vaulting shafts commonly rest upon this square abacus, with rather clumsy effect.

Arcades of single cylindrical columns occur at Notre-Dame Paris, Mouzon (Ardennes) and the Cathedral of Laon and were continued in Mid-Gothic in the beautiful example of Sées Cathedral (Orne) with slender vaulting-shafts attached. In other cases cylindrical columns alternate with massive piers to which half-columns are attached, as at Noyon Cathedral and Notre-Dame Mantes (Seine-et-Oise). Coupled columns occur at Sens Cathedral, and are frequent in early Gothic apses, as at Coutances Cathedral and Montierender (Hte.-Marne). The large column with four slender shafts attached was adopted at Chartres Cathedral, and thus a fashion was set which was followed at Amiens Cathedral and became a favourite later.

The arches of early Gothic churches retained the square-edged look of the earlier Romanesque style, and arch-mouldings in French Gothic were never so numerous, so varied or so deeply cut as in the corresponding development in England.

In the later Gothic and during the early inroads of Renaissance into the Gothic style, the abacus and capital tended to become insignificant, or to disappear altogether, and when this happened one of two methods of treatment was employed.

(*a*) Sometimes the arch-mouldings, were made to die away into a cylindrical pillar, as at St.-Étienne-du-Mont Paris, St.-Lô Valognes, and the churches of St.-Pierre and St.-Nicholas in Coutances (Manche), Villeneuve-le-Gayard and St.-Jean Joigny (Yonne).

(*b*) Or in other cases the mouldings of an arch were carried vertically down the pillar,[1] without the interruption of the horizontal line of abacus and capital. This method was followed in such examples as St.-Maclou Rouen, Mortagne (Orne), St.-Antoine Compiègne (Oise), St.-Ouen Pont-Audemer and Gisors (Eure), the church of the Madeleine Vendôme (Loir-et-Cher), St.-Thibault Joigny (Yonne), Arques-la-Bataille (Seine-Inférieure), St.-Wulfran and St.-Gilles Abbeville (Somme) and St.-Éloi (Dunkerque). Rarely in France late Gothic

[1] This was done also in some churches of the English Perpendicular style, as at Ormskirk (Lancs), Fowey and Lostwithiel (Cornwall).

pillars and arches were panelled all round without capitals[1] as at Château-du-Loir (Sarthe), but it was not uncommon in churches of Flamboyant design, or where late Gothic was merging into Renaissance, for pillars to be twisted, as at Gisors (Eure), Ste.-Croix Provins (Seine-et-Marne) and St.-Séverin Paris, or in exterior work at St.-Marc-la-Lande (Deux-Sèvres) and in transept portals as at Senlis Cathedral. At Gisors some pillars are curiously powdered with isolated ornaments and the like feature occurs on a smaller scale at Veules-les-Roses (Seine-Inférieure).

In the late Flamboyant style the form of arches, especially of portals sometimes reverted to a segmental or semi-circular shape, as in the façade at St.-Lô (Manche), and frequently in the portals of Breton churches, as at Ploërmel (Morbihan), Le Folgoët, Lampaul-Guimiliau and Tronoan (Finistère), as well as in windows, as at Notre-Dame Guingamp (Côtes-du-Nord), or in the arches of an interior arcade, as at St.-Herbot (Finistère). A like return to rounded forms of arch marked some work of the parallel late Perpendicular style in England, as at St.-Nicholas Gloucester, Bunbury and Malpas (Ches.) in windows, or in the arcade at Wybunbury (Ches.).

(2) Windows

As Gothic architecture advanced, its progress was marked by a great development in the fenestration of churches, the windows gradually increasing in size, as the art of stained glass demanded more and more scope for its exercise, and being filled with stone tracery of varied and beautiful forms.

[1] A similar panelling of pillars and arches occurs at Sherborne (Dorset) and was thence copied in other Dorset churches as at Charminster, Cerne, Abbotsbury, Portisham and St. Peter's Dorchester.

(A) The Growth of Window Tracery

In the early Gothic the windows were single lights as in the Romanesque style, but one of the first signs of actual transition in style was the making of the head of the window into a blunt point instead of a semi-circular form. These early lancet lights are seen in such churches as Noyon and Laon Cathedrals, Braisne (Aisne) and Mantes (Seine-et-Oise), at the east end of Pacy-sur-Eure (Eure), and in the west front at Mortain (Manche) and Gournay-en-Bray (Seine-Inférieure). In the last three cases the lancet-lights are arranged in a triplet. Similarly in the east end of St.-Georges-de-Bohon (Manche) a triplet of lancets is enclosed within a containing arch, and in the blank space between such coupled lancets in the choir of the same church a plain circular light is pierced, giving the simplest possible instance of what is called *plate tracery*. Similar examples occur at Quettehou (Manche), and at St.-Leu-d'Esserent (Oise), the last-named church having windows with a sexfoiled circle above a pair of lancets. St.-Léger Soissons (Aisne) shows in its choir and transepts three stages of progress from single lancets, through a two-light window with plate tracery of a foliated circle, to fully developed bar-tracery in a window of two lights with tracery of strictly geometrical form. Of this type were the windows of the great churches of the Gothic advance—Reims, Bourges, Amiens, Beauvais, the Ste.-Chapelle at Paris and its sister Ste.-Chapelle at St.-Germer (Oise)—and the French builders seem to have been so well satisfied with the effects obtained in their early Cathedrals that the form of window remained. Geometrical tracery of a rigid type and exhibiting little variety in form was thus

ALBI CATHEDRAL.

GOTHIC IN THE SOUTH.

facing p. 144.

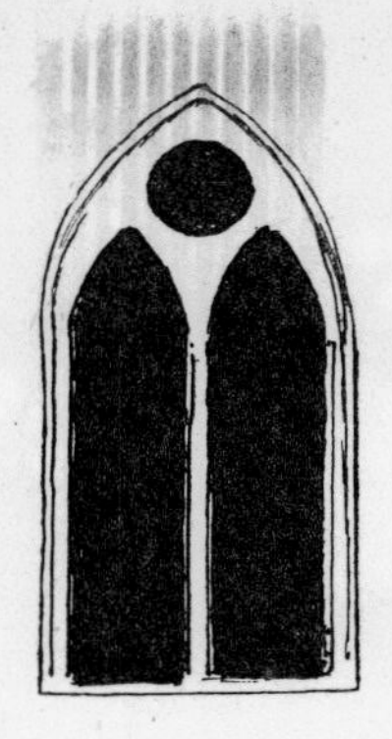

ST.-GEORGES-DE-BOHON (MANCHE).

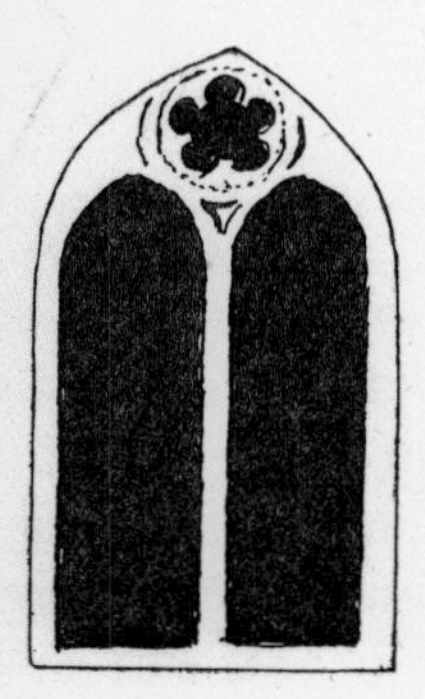

ST.-LÉGER SOISSONS (AISNE).

EVRON (MAYENNE).

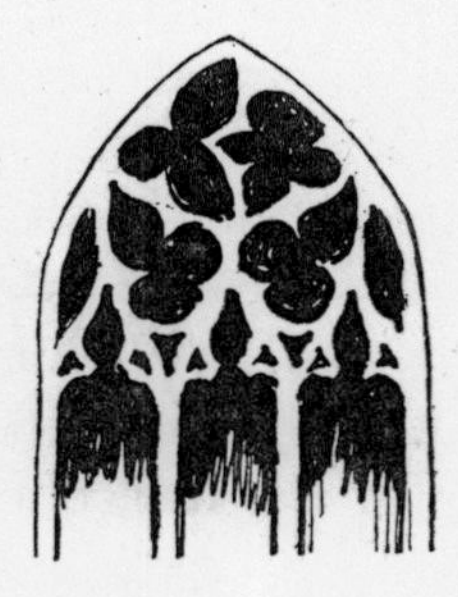

ST.-RÉMI TROYES.

DEVELOPMENT OF GOTHIC WINDOW TRACERY.

10

retained well on into the Mid-Gothic period, and right on to the fifteenth century.

The Mid-Gothic period of the fourteenth century was, however, also characterised by a development of more intricate geometrical tracery in the heads of windows which in façades were now often of many lights. Some excellent examples of fully developed *geometrical tracery* occur in the following churches :

St.-Julien Tours.
St.-Sulpice-de-Favières (Seine-et-Oise).
Dives (Calvados).
Coutances Cathedral (Manche).
Evron (Mayenne).
Puiseaux (Loiret).
St.-Satur (Cher).
Écouis and St.-Germain at Pont-Audemer (Eure).
Dormans (Marne).
Ennezat (Puy-de-Dôme).
St.-Antoine (Isère).
Marmande (Lot-et-Garonne).

In some cases the mullions of a window intersect in the head, producing tracery of a net-like or *reticulated* form. This is not very common in France, but good instances occur at Esnandes (Charente-Inférieure), Evron (Mayenne), the Abbey church of Souvigny (Allier) and the Kreisker church St.-Pol-de-Léon (Finistère).

So far window tracery ran a fairly parallel course in England and in France, except that the early type of strictly geometrical forms maintained a stronger hold in the latter country. But with the fifteenth century there came a marked divergence, which is registered in the names given to the latest phase of Gothic architecture in the two countries. While in England the lines of tracery stiffened into vertical lines, crossed at right-angles by transoms, which earned for the style the name of Perpendicular, the geometrical forms in France passed into waving lines giving flame-like openings, so that the late French Gothic is not inaptly termed *Flamboyant*. Perpendicular tracery is scarcely found

St.-Germain Pont-Audemer (Eure).

St.-Jean Troyes.

St.-Sauveur Dinan

St.-Taurin Évreux

Notre-Dame Le Havre.

Beaumont-le-Roger (Eure).

Late Gothic and Renaissance Window Tracery.

in France, but it occurs at Notre-Dame Calais, a town which was occupied by the English from the reign of Edward III to the time of Queen Mary. Similarly, of characteristic French Flamboyant work there is very little in England, the clearest examples being in Cornwall at Padstow, Lanteglos-by-Camelford and St.-Just-in-Penwith, where the forms of tracery are doubtless due to French influence, of which there are some other indications in the architecture of the county.[1]

Typical Flamboyant windows occur in very many places in France ; some of the best executed and most elaborate are at Ste.-Trinité Vendôme (Loir-et-Cher), St.-Germain Pont-Audemer and Le Grand-Andelys (Eure), St.-Wulfran Abbeville and St.-Ricquier (Somme), St.-Sauveur Dinan (Côtes-du-Nord), Caudebec-en-Caux (Seine-Inférieure) and the churches of St.-Maclou and St.-Vincent in Rouen. In a few cases window tracery assumes odd and ungainly forms, as in the church of St.-Rémi Troyes.

Just as in England heraldry entered a good deal into late Gothic decorative work, so also in France the window tracery was often so designed that the national heraldic badge of the fleur-de-lys occupied a central place, as in windows at St.-Rémi Troyes, Gennes (Maine-et-Loire), Graces (Côtes-du-Nord), St.-Sépulcre St.-Omer

[1] Bearing in mind that Scotland was, in the Middle Ages, long an ally of France, we are not surprised to find that Flamboyant tracery is not uncommon in the late Gothic churches of that country. It occurs in the large and important churches of Stirling, Linlithgow, Haddington and Melrose Abbey, and often in smaller churches, as at Seton Chapel near Prestonpans, Crichton and Mid-Calder, as well as at Roslyn Chapel, though the dominant influence in this last curious church seems to be Spanish. The French feature of a lofty apse at the east end also appears at Stirling and Linlithgow, and the occurrence of the gabled tower may be accounted a sign of French influence in the steeple of Dundee—tallest of Scottish towers—and the central towers at Crichton and Sweetheart Abbey Dumfries, the foundation of John Balliol and his wife.

(Pas-de-Calais) and Ste.-Marie-du-Mont (Manche). A parapet of pierced tracery with a series of fleurs-de-lys forms the cresting of the rood-screen at the church of the Madeleine Troyes, and Troyes Cathedral has on its façade a traceried parapet with design of the same *motif*.

The latest phase of French Gothic revelled in tracery, and pierced openings filled with the most delicate forms of it were by no means confined to windows. The parapets which crowned the towers or the side-walls of a church were pierced with lace-like openings of the most intricate patterns in which the characteristic, flame-like form was predominant.[1] Typical examples occur at St.-Germain and St.-Martin at Argentan (Orne), Gisors, Rugles and the Madeleine Verneuil-sur-Avre (Eure), and, in a great variety of patterns, at Ste.-Trinité Cherbourg (Manche), while at La-Ferté-Bernard (Sarthe) a very elaborate pierced parapet contains a long inscription in large letters. Screen gables of pierced tracery are often carried up in front of a façade or over a portal, as at Ste.-Trinité Vendôme, Louviers (Eure), Nôtre-Dame Alençon (Orne), St.-Germain Argentan and St.-Maclou Rouen. The aisle windows sometimes also have gables of pierced tracery above them,[2] intersecting

[1] In France the parapet of pierced tracery occupies the place held by the battlement in English churches. On the use of the battlement in France, see below, p. 214.

[2] This is like a reduction to skeleton form of the series of lateral gables presented by the north or south façade of a church when the aisles or a series of chapels are roofed transversely to the main roof of the church. We meet with such ranges of lateral gables at Bressuire (Deux-Sèvres), St.-Pargoire (Hérault), St.-Valéry-sur-Somme (Somme), Le-Tréport (Seine-Inférieure), St.-Lô and Carentan (Manche), Vitré (Ille-et-Vilaine), St.-Martin Lamballe (Côtes-du-Nord), the Kreisker church St.-Pol-de-Léon (Finistère), Ploërmel (Morbihan), St.-André (Aube), Fismes (Marne), St.-Gilles Étampes (Seine-et-Oise), St.-Bris (Yonne), St.-Pierre-des-Corps and Notre-Dame-la-Riche Tours, and St.-Vénérand Laval (Mayenne). The arrangement of the transverse gables is peculiar at Le-Ricey-Bas (Aube) in that the apex of each gable is set over a buttress instead of over

a parapet, as at Pont-de-l'Arche and Louviers (Eure). In the interior an effect of great richness is given by adorning the ribs of the vault with festoons or hanging fringes of lace-like or bead-like tracery, while long pendants hang from their intersections as at La-Ferté-Bernard (Sarthe), St.-Denis Poix and the exquisitely dainty Chapelle-du-Saint-Esprit at Rue (Somme).[1]

(B) The Design of Rose Windows

The distribution of rose windows has been already treated[2] and something may be said here about their design. The circular windows that were destined to play such an important part in French façade design began with plain round apertures in such Romanesque examples as St.-Sernin Toulouse and St.-Savin (Htes.-Pyrénées). From these were developed what may be called the wheel-window, the circular opening having radiating spokes inserted, generally in the form of small pillars with carved capitals. St.-Étienne Beauvais has in its north transept front a beautifully executed Romanesque example of this kind, Trie-Château (Oise) has one of similar design for the central feature of its west front and at St.-Contest (Calvados) is an early Gothic example of the same class. The western rose window at Chartres Cathedral is of a different type, being formed by a kind of plate tracery with pierced circles within its greater

a window as usual, and the church of Longpaon near Rouen is exceptional in having its lateral chapels covered by a series of separate hipped roofs making a curious façade on the north and south sides. Though an aisle roof with a series of transverse gables is thus not uncommon in France it is rarely met with in England, but examples are found at Horsham (Sussex), Enborne (Berks), Warblington (Hants) and Lugwardine (Hereford).

[1] Elaborately adorned vaults, with pendants, became more common when classical detail intruded into late Gothic. See below, p. 193.

[2] See above, pp. 15, 16.

circumference; a parallel to this may be found at Montréal (Yonne).

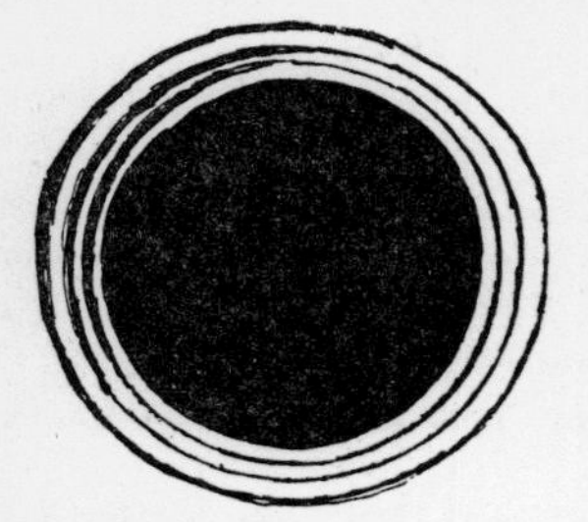

St.-Sernin Toulouse.

St.-Étienne Beauvais.

Pontigny (Yonne).

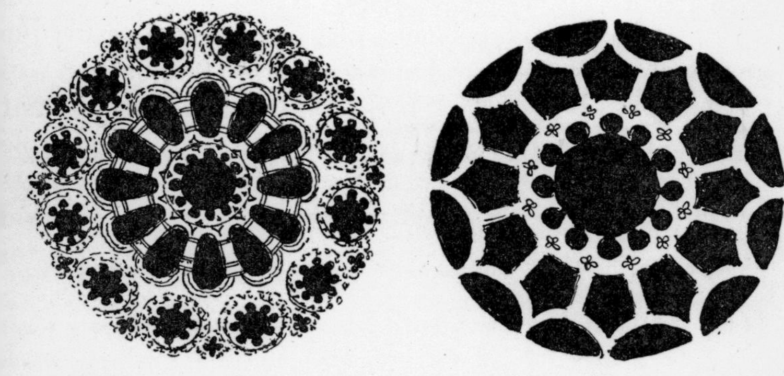

Chartres Cathedral. Laon Cathedral.

Designs of Rose Windows.

The next step in the development of the *rosaçe* was a mingling of geometrical forms around the circumference of a radiating design. To this type belong many splendid cathedral windows, besides some beautiful examples in other churches :

Chartres Cathedral (transept ends) of simple form.

The Cathedrals of Rouen (transept ends), Sées, Amiens, Soissons, Paris, Reims, Toulouse, Clermont-Ferrand, Orléans and Strasbourg.

The Saintes-Chapelles in Paris and at St.-Germer (Oise).

The churches of St.-Aignan Chartres, Notre-Dame Mantes (Seine-et-Oise), L'Epau (Sarthe), Braisne (Aisne), Vailly-sur-Aisne (Aisne), Cires-lès-Mello (Oise), Coulon (Deux-Sèvres), Notre-Dame Niort, St.-Nazaire Béziers (Hérault) and St.-Nazaire and St.-Michel at Carcassonne and St.-Ouen Rouen.

While some circular windows adopted radiating lines, others only had cusping round the circumference as an enrichment of their form, like the examples at Royat (Puy-de-Dôme), Pontigny (Yonne), Courmelles (Aisne) or Étaples (Pas-de-Calais).

In the Mid-Gothic period the radii tended to disappear from rose windows and the geometrical tracery, the full development of which was characteristic of the epoch, was arranged so as to fill the whole circle. Fine instances of geometric roses occur at :

St.-Pierre and St.-Étienne-le-Vieux Caen, Mello (Oise), Dreux (Eure-et-Loir), St.-Nicholas Blois (Loir-et-Cher), St.-Père-sous-Vezelay (Yonne), La-Rochefoucauld (Charente) the church of the Jacobins at Toulouse, Cahors Cathedral, St.-Vincent Carcassonne, St.-Jean-de-Malte at Aix-en-Provence, the Cathedral and St.-Bonaventure at Lyon, and St.-Laurent and the Carmelite church at Le Puy.

To these should be added a curious example in late Gothic at Ivry-la-Bataille (Eure), where the tracery consists entirely of plain small circles arranged within a larger circle.

The Rose Window developed into its greatest intricacy in the Flamboyant or latest phase of Gothic, yet at the same time there was more monotony in the shape of the openings of the design. Typical examples are :

Auxerre, Sens, Troyes, Amiens (west front), Senlis, Bordeaux, Rodez and Bayonne Cathedrals.

Of the vast number of churches which have *rosaçes* of this type a few may be singled out for mention, such as Saugnes (Hte.-Loire), Montferrand (Puy-de-Dôme), Le-Boupére and Chantonnay (Vendée), La-Mothe-St.-Heray (Deux-Sèvres), Le Grand-Andelys (Eure), St.-Jean Dijon, St.-Maclou Pontoise (Seine-et-Oise), St.-Maclou Rouen, Boisguillaume and Caudebec-en-Caux (Seine-Inférieure), Dunkerque and Bergues (Nord), Rue (Somme), St.-Antoine Compiègne and Chaumont-en-Vexin (Oise), St.-Michel Bordeaux and l'Église-de-la-Dalbade Toulouse. The fine *rosaçe* of the north transept of Notre-

Mello (Oise).

St.-Pierre Caen.

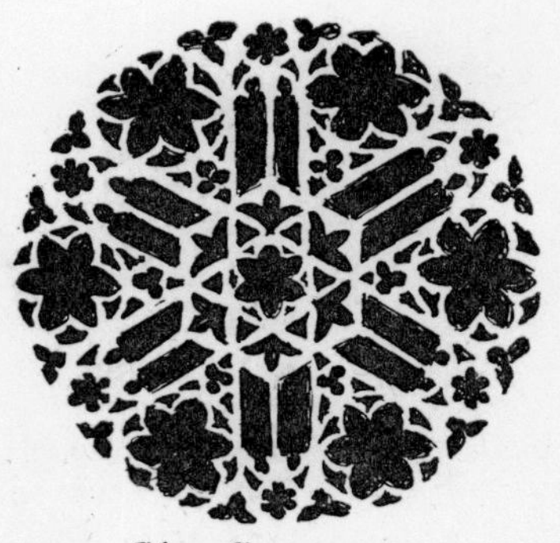

Sées Cathedral.

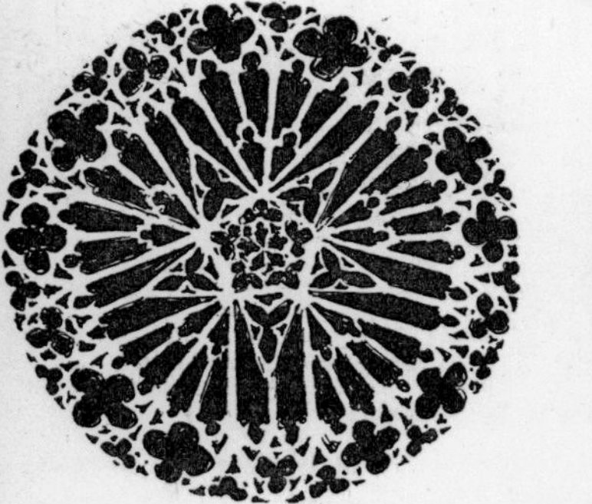

Amiens Cathedral.

Reims Cathedral.

Designs of Rose Windows.

St.-Ouen Rouen.

Notre-Dame St.-Omer (Pas-de-Calais).

Notre-Dame Le Havre.

Chaumont-en-Vexin (Oise).

Rouen Cathedral.

Designs of Rose Windows.

Dame St.-Omer (Pas-de-Calais) is noteworthy in having the fleur-de-lys for a centrepiece of its design of flowing tracery.

In the earlier phase of the Renaissance the traceried rose window was retained, and sometimes fitted with radiating spokes, as at St.-Rémi Dieppe, Le Grand-Andelys (Eure) and St.-Florentin (Yonne). In other cases, such as Évreux Cathedral (west front) and St.-Éustache and St.-Étienne-du-Mont in Paris, a clumsy attempt was made at flowing tracery. At Notre-Dame Le Havre is a small *rosaçe* with curved spokes and surrounded by a deeply undercut spiral wreath. In the later Renaissance where a circular window was used, it was a plain round aperture—thus singularly reverting to the earliest Romanesque form—surrounded either by a moulding as at the church of the Visitation at Le Mans and St.-Sauveur La Rochelle, or by a wreath as at St.-Louis Rouen.

(3) Portals

There are, here and there, examples of doorways of the early Gothic, or of the transition from Romanesque, of a simple and chaste type, with moulded arches and lateral shafts but without tympanum or figure sculpture. Ferrières (Loiret), Grand-Brassac (Dordogne), Mézin (Lot-et-Garonne), St.-Alpin Châlons-sur-Marne and Condé-en-Barrois (Meuse) have good doorways of this type. In the last case the head is semi-circular and the doorway as a whole resembles a bay of the arcade of St. Mary's Shrewsbury. But the typical French Gothic doorway is quite different from these.

In the south-east again are some doorways in the Italian manner, which had no influence beyond the border-land. Amongst such are the portal of Embrun Cathedral with the canopy supported by detached pillars resting upon lions, and a smaller doorway at Le Bar (Alpes-Maritimes) whose spiral shafts and arch-mouldings recall the design of portals at Siena and Orvieto.

The splendid portals of the fully developed and later Gothic with their horizontal lintels and wealth of figure sculpture are directly descended from the grand doorways of the earlier Romanesque and are amongst the most glorious of the special contributions of France to church architecture.

Cathedrals and greater churches usually have a range of three portals, occupying practically the whole of the lowest story of the façade, but this number is exceeded at Bourges, which has a magnificent range of five doorways on its western front.

The tympanum is in some cases blank, as at Le-Moutier-d'Ahun (Creuse), Chambéry (Savoie), St.-Pierre Avignon and Carpentras (Vaucluse), but is in early and Mid-Gothic examples usually filled with figure-sculpture of the finest character, while statuary flanks the doorway on either side and is carried, with tabernacle work, round the arch above. The great portals of Notre-Dame Paris and the Cathedrals of Chartres (transept façades), Reims and Amiens are of surpassing beauty and grandeur and renowned for the extraordinary excellence of their figure sculpture. The Romanesque sculpture on tympana and on capitals had been abstract in character and conventional in form with an indifference to reality, the tympana being filled with such subjects as Christ enthroned amid the living creatures of the Apocalypse,[1] or the Last Judgment as at Conques (Aveyron) and at the Cathedral of Autun. But Gothic sculpture from the thirteenth century onwards evidenced a brilliant revival of realism, natural foliage appeared upon capitals, as in the celebrated vintage capital of Reims, and motives are taken from the animal and vegetable kingdom, the seasons of the year, their corresponding occupations and the arts and crafts of man. The perfect Gothic sculpture shows close affinity with the Greek of 500 to 450 B.C., the difference being that in Gothic work the figures are draped. Though realism marks this best period of Gothic sculpture, it is remarkable that it does not dwell upon the sufferings of Christ or of the Saints. Christ is figured

[1] See above, p. 72.

in serene majesty, not tortured upon the Cross, and there is no Virgin weeping at the foot of the Cross. The story of scripture and the drama of Redemption is not treated in a sentimental way on its human side, but episodes are rather illustrated because of their bearing upon Christian doctrine. Thus the great portals contain a summary of the Faith, a cyclopædia of scripture, the legends of the saints and of human knowledge, with moral allegories and personifications of virtues and vices. Unusually well-designed and executed scenic sculpture fills the tympanum in some lesser-known churches. The Resurrection of the Dead at the Last Judgment is thus finely depicted at Larchant (Seine-et-Marne), and the coronation of Our Lady in sculpture of much dignity and distinction occupies the tympanum at Longpont-sous-Montlhéry (Seine-et-Oise). A later doorway at La-Neuville-sous-Corbie (Somme) has for its subject in the like position the triumphal entry of Our Lord into Jerusalem, executed with a great deal of careful and effective detail. As the great majority of western doorways and transept portals have double doors, the tympanum beneath the wide enclosing arch gives ample scope for such figure sculpture as has just been described.

As the Gothic style developed, connected subjects in the tympanum or groups of figure sculpture gave place to a range of canopied niches for statuary. This type of design is found at St.-Antoine (Isère), Ste.-Radigonde Poitiers, Ménigoute (Deux-Sèvres), St.-Léonard Honfleur (Calvados), Beauvais Cathedral, Cahors Cathedral (west doorway), St.-Maurice Vienne (Isère), Gisors north transept portal (Eure), Arcis-sur-Aube, Jully-sur-Sarce and Pont-sur-Seine (Aube) and Sens Cathedral (transept).

In late Gothic façades and portals there is an elaboration and multiplication of canopies and tabernacle-work, while figure sculpture and statuary take a secondary place or are practically absent. This tendency is observable in such churches as the Cathedrals of Auxerre, Meaux and Troyes, St.-Étienne Toul, St.-Wulfran Abbeville, St.-Ricquier and the Chapelle-St.-Esprit at Rue (Somme).

Portals worthy of study in churches other than those above referred to occur at :

The Cathedrals of Laon (early), Rouen, Sées, Poitiers, Bordeaux, Évreux, Nantes and Bazas (Gironde), Dax (Landes), Anet (Eure-et-Loir), Mont-Richard (Loir-et Cher), St.-Mard and Vailly-sur-Aisne (Aisne), Norrey (transept) and St.-Pierre Caen (Calvados), Caudebec-en-Caux (Seine-Inférieure), St.-Père-sous-Vézelay (Yonne) and Chaumont-en-Vexin (Oise).

The Flamboyant or late Gothic was characterised, as has been already noted, by a fondness for pierced tracery and this tendency towards open-work for adornment of wall-space was extended to the tympanum of a doorway in an example as early as the west doorway of Reims, where the tympanum is filled with glazed tracery of *rosaçe* form. Eventually it became quite a regular feature of late Gothic style to substitute a traceried window for the solid tympanum in the head of a doorway.

Examples are seen at the Cathedrals of Albi (south porch), Limoges, Auch, Tours, Soissons (north doorway) and Quimper, and graceful ones also occur at Ligugé (Vienne), St.-Marc-la-Lande (Deux-Sèvres), St.-Wulfran and St.-Gilles Abbeville (Somme), Beaumont-le-Roger (Eure), Guérande (Loire-Inférieure), Ste.-Catherine-de-Fierbois (Indre-et-Loire), the Chapel of the castle at Amboise, with exquisite sculpture of the legend of St.-Hubert and the Stag, and Ile-Bouchard (Indre-et-Loire), Ste.-Trinité and the Lycée Chapel at Vendôme

(Loir-et-Cher), Bernay, Louviers, Le Grand-Andelys and Gisors (Eure). The great west doorway at St.-

Ervy (Aube).

Ricquier is of unusual beauty and is peculiar in having the tracery in its head designed in the form of a

Tree of Jesse, with finely executed figures on a small scale.[1]

It is, however, in the Department of Aube that the tympanum of glazed tracery most frequently occurs, and a great many of the smaller churches in this part of the country have beautifully designed doorways of the kind such as those at Ervy, Laines-aux-Bois, Bouilly, St.-Phal, St.-André, Pont-Ste-Marie, l'Huitre, Bar-sur-Seine and Polisot, all in the Department of Aube. In some cases statuary is effectively set as a centrepiece to the traceried window, as at Bouilly, St.-André, l'Huitre and Bar-sur-Seine.

(4) The Design of Towers

The early Gothic towers at first carried on the Romanesque tradition in their fenestration, and two types may be distinguished :

(*a*) The belfry windows take the form of two small lights placed close together, separated only by a shaft and enclosed within a containing arch. Well-designed examples with a simple dignity may be seen at Lillers (Pas-de-Calais) and St.-Germain Pont-Audemer (Eure) while at Angy (Oise) are similar lights of great beauty with plate tracery of trefoil form in the head.

(*b*) Or the whole tower is taken up with a succession of short stages of arcading after the manner of such Romanesque towers as those of Angoulême Cathedral and St.-Sernin Toulouse. The fine tower of Château-Landon (Seine-et-Marne) exhibits this type of design, and has three stages with long open lancets, arranged two on each face.

But early in the Gothic style the lancet lights were lengthened, so that the upper part of the tower, often

[1] There is a parallel to this adoption of the Tree of Jesse for the design of the tracery of a window in the choir at Dorchester (Oxon).

BOURGES CATHEDRAL.

facing p. 160.

the whole of it that appeared above the roof of the church, was made to consist of one stage only, with immensely long open lights, generally two on each face of the tower, that were sometimes fitted with louvre-boards. This is the characteristically French[1] type of tower that seems to preside with queenly grace alike over cathedrals and greater churches such as Noyon, Laon, Notre-Dame Mantes, Notre-Dame Paris and Reims Cathedral, over lesser churches as at Champeau (Seine-et-Marne) and Corbeil (Seine-et-Oise) and with inimitable stateliness and simplicity occurs as a central tower in village churches of rare beauty at Dormans[2] (Marne) and Augy and Ambléný (Aisne).

The type of tower design just discussed was specially taken up in Normandy in the Mid-Gothic period and with the addition of a stone spire was developed into a beautiful steeple which became a great favourite in the whole of that part of France. The features of this steeple group may be briefly described as follows:

(1) Each face of the tower is occupied by four tall pointed openings, the two centre ones open for lights and filled in with simple geometrical tracery in their heads, the two lateral ones much narrower and blind.

(2) From within a pierced parapet and masked by well-developed angle pinnacles rises the octagonal spire.

(3) The spire itself received an elaborate treatment. The early spires, which have been already referred to

[1] The towers of Lincoln Cathedral belong to the same class in design and arrangement of belfry-lights, and for grace of form are among the first in England, but they stand practically alone as English examples of the elongated belfry-stage. Lincoln has some other remarkable affinities with French church architecture, as, for example, the large *rosaçes* forming the centrepieces of its transept fronts.

[2] Dormans is distinct from the other towers mentioned in having three tall lancets on each face of its tower.

as natural to the round-arched style,[1] were sometimes covered with an incised ornament resembling overlapping scales or small tiles,[2] or in some cases early spires had been covered with incised horizontal lines, as at Bayeux Cathedral. In some early Gothic spires incised ornament of the kind was arranged in horizontal bands, as at the Abbaye-aux-Hommes Caen, Audrieu, Bernières and Douvres (Calvados). In the Mid-Gothic period the incised patterns became more elaborate, were varied on the same spire and arranged in horizontal bands, the whole surface being covered, as in the beautiful examples at St.-Pierre Caen and Carentan (Manche). The rich effect was still further increased by pierced openings, generally referred to as "wind-holes," of geometrical form—sexfoil, cinquefoil, quatrefoil, trefoil or circular (all these forms occur in the one example of St.-Pierre Caen)—in diminishing scale as they ascend as at St.-Sauveur Caen, Carentan and Notre-Dame St.-Lô (Manche). The intricacy of outline is still further enhanced by crockets that give a serrated appearance to the angles of the spire.

Of this type of steeple St.-Pierre Caen stands as the great example, and is acknowledged to be one of the most perfect architectural works of Europe. Scarcely inferior are the tower and spire of St.-Sauveur in the same city. Other instances are numerous in the Department of Calvados, as at Audrieu, Ducy, Bernières, Norrey (with spire truncated), Langrune, Fierville, Mézières, Rouvres, Bazanville, Vierville and Louvières. The twin western spires of the Cathedrals of St.-Pol-de-Léon and Quimper (Finistère) are of the same class, as is also (though rather later in date) the magnificent and tall steeple of Notre-Dame de Kreisker at St.-Pol-de-Léon.

[1] See above, p. 91. [2] See above, pp. 91, 92.

In other districts spire ornament took other forms. There is a notable group of handsome stone spires on and near the Biscay coast, which are banded at intervals with a chevron on each face, as at Notre-Dame Niort, Notre-Dame and St.-Jean Fontenay-le-Comte (Vendée), Moëze and Ars-en-Ré (Charente-Inférieure), and in an attenuated form at the Cathedral of Luçon, a later example.

St.-Pierre Caen.

The district of the Somme and Pas-de-Calais is also characterised by the prevalence of stone spires somewhat heavily crocketed, though as a rule small in scale, and pierced by many wind-holes of loophole or circular form. Typical examples are at Fontaine-sur-Somme, Longpré and Lumbres (Somme)

CARENTAN (MANCHE).

and St.-Sépulcre St.-Omer and Arques (Pas-de-Calais)

During the prevalence of the later Gothic steeples

with handsome crocketed spires were built in various parts of France and are independent of local architectural influence. Grand examples of the kind occur at Notre-Dame-d'Avénières Laval (Mayenne), St.-Malo (Ille-et-Vilaine), St.-Maixent (Deux-Sèvres), St.-Pierre (truncated) and St.-Eutrope at Saintes and Marennes (Charente-Inférieure), the Cathedrals of Mende (two dissimilar steeples) and Tulle (without crockets), Bordeaux Cathedral with curious pear-shaped wind-holes, St.-Michel Bordeaux, Bazas and St.-Émilion (Gironde), Harfleur and Lillebonne (Seine-Inférieure) and Hondschoote (Nord).

The general tendency of the early Gothic towards slenderness of form showed itself in the employment of detached shafts. These are grouped on the towers of Laon Cathedral and on the south-west tower of Senlis, so as to form angle buttresses of open-work. The appearance of the design, especially at Senlis, suggests that it is a development from earlier Romanesque angle pinnacles which were sometimes constructed of a conical cap standing on a diminutive open arcade as at Ste.-Trinité Vendôme (Loir-et-Cher) or Notre-Dame Étampes (Seine-et-Oise). At any rate the airy grace of such an arrangement appealed to the French Gothic builders and we find it adopted in a most striking manner for the western towers of the Cathedral at Reims. Detached shafts are also employed in similar fashion to mask the angles of the top stage of the beautiful tower at St.-Père-sous-Vézelay (Yonne). In the late Gothic of the north-east the angle buttresses have open-work in spiral form corresponding to the lines of the staircase contained within, as at Strasbourg Cathedral and St.-Thiébault Thann (Haut-Rhin), and this feature appears in the tallest of towers of similar type at Ulm in Würtemberg.

LAON CATHEDRAL.

The tendency of the Flamboyant style to substitute screens of pierced tracery for other decoration, which

ST.-MACLOU ROUEN.

has already been commented on, was extended to spire design. The ornamentation of the spire, which earlier consisted of bands of carved decoration, was pierced, as at St.-Maclou Rouen, and that eventually to such an extent as to leave only the crocketed angle ribs as a

NOTRE-DAME-DE-L'ÉPINE (MARNE).

skeleton frame-work girt about with ornamental bands as at Notre-Dame-de-l'Épine (Marne), or girdled with a triple crown and tracery as in the beautiful example at Caudebec-en-Caux (Seine-Inférieure). More often the spaces between the ribs of the spire were filled in with a network of open tracery, as at St.-Nizier Lyon and St.-Maurice Lille. Such spire of open tracery became characteristic of late Continental Gothic and travelled far. We find it at Ste.-Gertrude Louvain, at Strasbourg Cathedral, St.-Thiébault Thann (Haut-Rhin), in great churches of German Gothic at Cologne, Ulm, Ratisbon, Freiburg-im-Breisgau, the Frauenkirche Esslingen and the Michaeliskirche Breslau, in Switzerland at Berne and as far south as Burgos and Léon in Spain. Iron is perhaps a more suitable material than stone for such class of structure, and was employed with great effect for the spire of open-work added in the last century to the central tower of Rouen Cathedral.

The square pinnacled tower without spire or other finish, which is especially characteristic of English church architecture, is not very common in France, but good examples in the Flamboyant style occur at St.-Jacques Paris, St.-André Rouen, Darnétal, St.-Jacques Dieppe, St.-Étienne Fécamp (Seine-Inférieure), the Abbey of Bec (Eure), Notre-Dame, St.-Denis and St.-Bertin at St.-Omer, Aire-sur-la-Lys (Pas-de-Calais), Dunkerque (Nord) and Auxerre and Sens Cathedrals. Frequently a tower terminates in a pierced parapet, as at St.-Vincent Rouen and St.-Nizier Troyes, though in such cases pinnacles seem to have been intended. Some of these late Gothic towers are panelled all over—like the English Perpendicular towers of Gloucester, Evesham and Malvern—as at the churches of St.-Omer and Aire-sur-la-Lys in the north, or completely veiled with ranges of canopied niches as in the splendid examples at Troyes, Auxerre, Nevers and Rodez Cathedrals and at Clameçy (Nièvre).

A superimposed octagon upon a square tower gives

The Abbey of St.-Bertin St.-Omer (Pas-de-Calais).

a very satisfactory outline and a pleasing finish. Such arrangement is found in very early Romanesque in the western towers at Jumièges, and in the expiring Gothic

St.-Ouen Rouen.

of Orléans Cathedral. The central tower of St.-Ouen at Rouen is one of the best known, as it is one of the most graceful specimens in the world of this type of design. In spite of Ruskin's criticism of the great angle pinnacles as "four idle servants," most will agree with Professor Freeman in his enthusiastic admiration

Rugles (Eure).

of "the inimitable St.-Ouen's," and perhaps worthy of mention with it is the detached Tour-Pey-Berland at Bordeaux Cathedral whose octagon stage is capped with a blunt spire. The south-west tower of the Cathedral at Rouen is another example of very rich design with octagonal upper story. A local type in Normandy also exhibits an octagon story of small proportions, surmounting a large and ornate square tower, as at St.-Laurent Rouen, Rugles (Eure) and the church of the Madeleine Verneuil-sur-Avre (Eure), the last-named a fruit of this great tower-building era of the latest Gothic worthy to be compared with its sister "Magdalen" tower of the same period at Oxford. But these last-mentioned Flamboyant towers, like the tower at Laigle (Orne), not far distant, are dripping with lace-like tracery, in contrast to the rigid lines of English Perpendicular style. In the north-east of France some towers occur where the upper octagonal stage is of larger proportion than in the Normandy towers just referred to, and the effect is very fine in the western

St.-Michel-aux-Lions Limoges.

towers at St.-Étienne Toul, St.-Léon Nancy and Pont-à-Mousson (Meurthe-et-Moselle).

A still loftier octagonal stage upon a square tower was the local fashion in Limoges. But these towers at Limoges Cathedral and the churches of St.-Pierre and St.-Michel-aux-Lions form a class apart. Upon a square base—in the case of the cathedral the broad-spreading base of an earlier western tower—rise four slender angle turrets which run up to the top of the tower, and within these the tower is octagonal (in three stories at the Cathedral and St.-Michel, in two at St.-Pierre), but this octagon stage is oddly set, one of its angles being engaged in each turret, and one bisecting each side of the square below. At St.-Michel as well as at St.-Pierre the whole finishes with a spire and four sharply-pointed pinnacles, and the effect must be pronounced very good.

St.-Didier Avignon.

Another local type of tower design in which an octagonal stage plays a part is that of Avignon and its district. Amongst the church towers of Avignon a common character prevails. Upon the tower stands a story of open arches, less in area than the tower below and crowned by a blunt but boldly crocketed spire. The open story is generally octagonal, as at St.-Agricole, St.-Didier and St.-Pierre, but square in the Hôtel-de-Ville belfry of kindred design. Other towers of the same kind may be seen in the neighbourhood along the Rhône valley, and St.-Marthe at Tarascon shows the type on a large scale. The Avignon towers have something of an Italian look about them corresponding to the Gothic of Cremona or Verona rather than to that of Amiens or Reims, and the bells in some of them are hung, in Italian fashion, in the outer walls.

There yet remain to be considered the different fashions of tower-finish, where there is no stone covering of spire form. First of these forms should be mentioned the Gabled Tower. This is widely distributed on the Continent and occurs alike in Romanesque and Gothic buildings. Its prevalence in Normandy and especially in the Department of Calvados has been already referred to.[1] In the Romanesque of Germany the characteristic finish of the tower is the four-gabled form crowned with a blunt four-sided spire. Typical examples of this "German helm," as it has been called, are at the Abbey church of Laach, the Apostles' Church Cologne, and the Cathedral of Limburg-am-Lahn, while England can show one tower of the kind in the pre-Conquest Romanesque at Sompting (Sussex). When the gabled form of finish was adopted by the Gothic builders two sides of the tower only were usually terminated with a gable, giving the form known as "saddleback." Four-gabled towers were less frequently adopted in the Gothic style, and where they occur they are almost always central towers. "Saddleback" towers on the other hand are found in every variety

[1] See above, pp. 94–96.

of position, sometimes central or lateral and occasionally western. It seems to be a general rule that when the tower is central or western the east and west sides of it are carried up into gables, so that the ridge of the tower roof is in line with that of the church below, as at Ryes and Formigny (Calvados), St.-Céneri-le-Gerei (Orne) and St.-Georges-de-Bohon (Manche). Where, however, the tower is lateral the north and south sides are most frequently the gabled ones, so that the ridge runs at right angles to the roof-ridge of the church, as at Mouen and Maisoncelles-la-Jourdan (Calvados), St.-Sauveur-le-Vicomte and Biville (Manche). In the great majority of cases the gable has the form of an equilateral triangle, but sometimes it is of steeper isosceles form, as at Formigny and Verson (Calvados).

The gabled form of finish seems to have been cultivated in France for its own sake [1] and is frequently met with in Gothic churches, sometimes in an ornamented form and on a grand scale. The still more elaborate four-gabled form is also fairly common, the tower roof finishing in ridges running horizontally from the points of the opposite gables, and intersecting in the centre, the whole being in some cases crowned effectively with a slender *flèche* at the intersection. Towers of this type occur from Dormans (Marne) in the east to Guibray (Calvados), Ranes (Orne), Tocqueville (Manche) and La-Ferté-Bernard (Sarthe), and they vary in design from the stern severity of Ranes to the elaborate late Gothic of La-Ferté-Bernard. The district north of Paris, covered by the Departments of Oise, Aisne and Marne is particularly rich in these towers, some four-

[1] In England the gabled tower seems to have been deliberately cultivated only on the borders of Oxon and Bucks and on the line of the old Banbury and Northampton road. Elsewhere it seems to be a makeshift finish, when the tower has not been completed as was originally intended.

BOURGES CATHEDRAL.

facing p. 176.

gabled as at Dormans (Marne), Braisne and Augy (Aisne), some saddleback as at Créteil, Nogent-les-Vierges and Angy (Oise) and Ambléný, Ciry-Salsogne

Dormans (Marne).

and Venizel (Aisne). The prevalence of the four-gabled pattern in this part of France is probably due to the fact that the fashion was set by the central tower of the Abbey of Ste.-Marie in Soissons, destroyed at the Revolution, for the architecture of a great religious house naturally influenced the style of churches over a wide area around. Old pictures of Ste.-Marie at Soissons show a well-proportioned four-gabled tower, with lights in the gables above the main belfry lights, and with a *flèche* similar to the one at Braisne.

The carrying up of each side of the tower into a

AMBLÉNY (AISNE).

gable is, as has been noted above, a characteristic feature of the German Romanesque, and its presence in the neighbourhood of Soissons is probably due to influence from that quarter, an inference corroborated by the presence of apsidal transepts in the German manner at Soissons and Noyon Cathedrals.[1] But though the adoption of the gabled tower finish may be

[1] See above, p. 103.

one of several signs of German influence in the district the manner in which it has been treated is thoroughly French. The towers often have the long open lights of the French early Gothic, as at Dormans, Augy and Ambléeny, and there are lights in the gables—lancets

AUGY (AISNE).

with quatrefoiled circle above at Braisne, trefoiled lancets and three foliated circles at Ambléeny, a traceried circle at Angy, and in the finely crocketed gables at Augy elaborate geometrical tracery like the head of large window.

A gabled tower, whether four-gabled or saddleback, presents a good outline, and is almost always pleasing in effect, so that even when the towers are neither lofty nor richly adorned they seem dignified and appropriate, and the surrounding buildings group with them in a manner that is thoroughly satisfactory to the eye, as at Droizy and Venizel.

Of less usual forms of tower finish the *hipped roof* is fairly common in the north-western part of France. When this is employed, as is the case also with gabled towers, the tower is not finished, strictly speaking, after the manner of a tower, but in a fashion usual for the roofing of other structures such as houses or the body of a church. The hipped form of tower roof is found on a large scale at the north-west tower, or Tour St.-Romain at Rouen Cathedral, and frequently occurs in parochial churches in Normandy, as at Envermeu, St.-Rémi Dieppe and Arques-la-Bataille (Seine-Inférieure). It is also the form adopted for the very gorgeous late Gothic tower at Laigle (Orne), for the western towers at Écouis (Eure) and at St.-Leu in Amiens. Sometimes the hipped roof springs from within a parapet, as at Rouen Cathedral, Laigle and Écouché (Orne), but often it is placed upon a tower after the manner of a simple roof with eaves as at Écouis and Arques-la-Bataille.

When towers are completed with timber spires these are slated, shingled or leaded. Spires of this class are sometimes very picturesque, or even fantastic, in their outline, as at St.-Jean Laigle (Orne) and Nonancourt (Eure), and they are often fitted with louvre-boards in their lower part as at Boisguillaume and Gournay-en-Bray (Seine-Inférieure) and Mello (Oise). It is a drawback that the timber frame-work of such spires may become warped so that the spire leans or becomes distorted, as in the curious twisted example at Puiseaux (Loiret), which may be compared to

Chesterfield spire in England, and with the still more aggravated case at Mayen in Rhenish Prussia.

ARQUES-LA-BATAILLE (SEINE-INFÉRIEURE).

Leaded spires are often ornamentally treated, openings in them being surmounted by little crocketed gables and flanked by pinnacles. The fine western spires of Notre-Dame Châlons-sur-Marne show this treatment. In the

NOTRE-DAME, VERNEUIL-SUR-AVRE (EURE).

later Gothic we sometimes meet with a leaded spire or superstructure, elaborate or even fantastic in design, as at Notre-Dame, Verneuil-sur-Avre (Eure); and a *flèche* for a bell upon a tower became a very ornate structure taking the form of an open cage with tracery, a forest of

Nonancourt (Eure).

buttresses and pinnacles and a maze of flying buttresses. Évreux Cathedral has a fine spirelet of this kind upon its central tower, and the belfry of the same city bears a picturesque leaded cage on its summit containing a large bell. The church tower of Conches in the same neighbourhood has a loftier and more intricate open cage or spirelet of similar design.

The valley of the Loire and its neighbourhood, especially about Orléans, is marked by a local form of tower finish in which a pyramidal roof is surmounted by a slender *flèche* that has an opening at its base for a bell. This characteristic form of spire occurs at St.-Benoît-sur-Loire and Gien (Loiret), Anet (Eure-et-Loire), St.-Nicholas Blois (Loir-et-Cher), Bérulles (Aube), Gargilesse (Indre), St.-Parize-le-Châtel (Nièvre) and elsewhere in this part of France.

A slender spire or bell-*flèche* is quite usual in the village churches over a large part of northern France, especially in Normandy, and in some larger churches it occurs where there is no tower, as at Le Petit-Andelys (Eure) and Montreuil-Bellay (Maine-et-Loire), or it occupies a central position on the roof-ridge where the tower is detached, as at Ste.-Trinité Vendôme (Loir-et-Cher), or where the tower is lateral, as at Caudebec-en-Caux (Seine-Inférieure) and the Cathedral of Nevers. Lofty and gracefully designed leaded *flèches* stand above the crossing of great cathedrals where there is no central tower, as at Amiens, Dijon and Orléans. At Reims a similar *flèche* is perched somewhat oddly at the extreme east end of the long roof, a position imitated in the Renaissance church of St.-Eustache Paris, while at Tours Cathedral the central *flèche*, like the pair of western towers, has a cupola finish.

Wooden and slated, or leaded, forms of tower finish, especially when they are of makeshift character, often assume a domical shape in France, as seen in such instances as St.-Saturn Blois, St.-Jean Verneuil-sur-

Avre (Eure), St. Quiriace Provins, St.-Gilles Abbeville, St.-Sever (Calvados), and the smaller churches of Breuil and Ecajeul in the same Department, and Bourbourg (Nord). St.-Sauveur Dinan (Côtes-du-Nord) is peculiar in having three superimposed domes of diminishing scale by way of a spire, recalling the steeples with piled up bulbous forms that are characteristic of the Netherlands.

(5) Fittings and Accessories

The later Gothic period was the Golden Age of church furniture, and from the fifteenth century and the earlier part of the sixteenth date most of the splendid rood-screens, stalls and other woodwork with which churches in general were fitted. Much fine work of the kind perished in France at the Revolution, and the rage for vistas which marked the earlier half of the nineteenth century in France and England alike was responsible for clearing away many of the remaining rood-screens.

Some fine examples of rood-screens, nevertheless, are still in existence. Most of these are executed in wood, as at the Cathedrals of Albi and Auch, at Condom (Gers), Moulineaux (Seine-Inférieure), Villemaur (Aube) and Lynde (Nord). In Brittany especially rood-screens have remained undisturbed, and examples of great beauty with intricate Flamboyant tracery occur at Tonquedec (Côtes-du-Nord), the Chapelle of St.-Fiacre at Le Faoüet and Notre-Dame-de-Quelven Guern (Morbihan), Lambader, Kerfons and St.-Herbot (Finistère). Rood-screens of stone are less common. The church of the Madeleine Troyes has a late Flamboyant one of the greatest beauty, and there are other fine ones at Notre-Dame-de-l'Épine (Marne),

St.-Florentin (Yonne) and the church of Brou near Bourg (Ain). The Abbey church of La-Chaise-Dieu (Hte.-Loire) has a rood-screen of stone designed with much simplicity and dignity, and at Le Folgoët (Finistère) is a pleasing one of small scale executed in the local material of granite.

Stalls of great beauty with spire-like canopies are in the choir of Amiens Cathedral, and a ritual choir is formed in the Cathedral of Albi and the church of Condom (Gers) by screen-work and stalls of most delicate tracery and canopy-work. Stalls of unusual grandeur are also found at Le-Moutier-d'Ahun (Creuse), Auch Cathedral (Gers), St.-Claude Cathedral (Jura), La-Chaise-Dieu (Hte.-Loire) and Brou (Ain). Fine stalls occur besides at Le-Puy-Notre-Dame and Les-Ponts-de-Cé (Maine-et-Loire), Vendôme (Loir-et-Cher), Toulouse Cathedral, St.-Jean-de-Maurienne (Savoie), St.-Étienne Beauvais, St. Pierre-sur-Dives (Calvados), St.-Pol-de-Léon Cathedral and St.-Thiébault Thann (Haut-Rhin).

Of other screen-work of the later Gothic period the stone carving of the *partour-du-chœur* at Amiens and at Chartres is world-famous and quite unsurpassed for the interest and beauty of the sculpture, and for the delicacy of canopies, crockets, and finials. There are similar screens of equal beauty in the transepts also at Amiens. The screens of woodwork to the lateral chapels at Évreux Cathedral are probably the finest of their kind, and are remarkable for the variety of Flamboyant design they exhibit in their tracery.

In connexion with the subject of woodwork in churches a very remarkable feature of the ecclesiology of the Pyrénées district should not be overlooked. Aisleless churches there are sometimes fitted with balustraded galleries arranged along the side-walls in two or three tiers and reserved for the use of men during service-time. This curious arrangement is well exemplified in the churches of St.-Jean-de-Luz, Ciboure, Ainhoue and Hendaye (Basses-Pyrénées), and we meet with it again at the strange fortified church of Les-Saintes-Maries (Bouches-du-Rhône), which has one long gallery of similar type.

Delicately carved reredoses of great beauty occur at Rumilly-les-Vaudes (Aube), St.-Pierre Vic-sur-Cère (Cantal) and a splendid one in alabaster at Montréal (Yonne). One at Chaource (Aube) has the legend of St.-Hubert for its subject, and the Crucifixion forms the centre panel of fine examples at Maiguelay (Oise) and Lawarde-Mauger (Somme).

Carved doors of excellent execution belonging to the late Gothic or early Renaissance style are not uncommon, and specimens of unusual beauty are found at the Cathedral of Aix-en-Provence, Beauvais Cathedral, St.-Wulfran Abbeville (by Gilles Amourette *c.* 1550), St.-Maclou Rouen and Beaumont-le-Roger (Eure), of Flamboyant design. The finest Renaissance doors are at Utelle (Alpes-Maritimes) and St.-Pierre Avignon (in walnut by Volard, 1551).

CHAPTER VII

RENAISSANCE

(1) The Renaissance in Western Europe

After running its course of development for three hundred years the pointed architecture of western Europe began, in the fifteenth century, to show marks of decadence. Amid all the splendour of the French Flamboyant, as also of the English Perpendicular, there was a great deal of work that was meagre, unsatisfying and poorly executed. The lines of a building were sometimes thin and wiry, and it was a sign of weakness that the very gorgeousness which the latest phase of Gothic architecture exhibits was sometimes attained by a meaningless repetition of identical forms in panelling, tabernacle-work, parapets of open tracery and the like. Men's minds were ready for a change, and the change came from Italy, following in the wake of the revival of learning. The renewed interest in the literature of ancient Greece and Rome in time naturally affected the various departments of life. In religion it sent men back to the reading of the Greek Testament and to the writings of the early Christian Fathers, and opened the way for the changes of the Reformation. In architecture and art the new movement brought a change of taste.

Gothic architecture had never obtained in Italy the strong hold that it had upon the peoples farther north and west, and in that country the revival of classic taste in art took place so rapidly that, without any transition period, there was a reversion from Mediævalism, alike in painting, sculpture and architecture, to the form and style of antique compositions, statues and architectural remains.

Brunelleschi, who designed the great dome of the Cathedral at Florence, was the leading exponent of the Renaissance in architecture and began his work as early as the middle of the fifteenth century. His buildings, in which severe and pure classic details are employed, struck a keynote that had been responded to all over Italy before the close of the century.

(2) The First Phase of Renaissance Style—A Blending of Classic Detail with Late Gothic Plan and General Conception

To other countries the change in architectural taste spread later, and it was not welcomed in the same unreserved manner. "Renaissance," after all, is not perhaps a very good name for the style to which it is given, for the term would seem to imply that art was dead and then revived again to appear in its old form, whereas the spirit of classical art was in fact modified by ten centuries of Christian influence, so that it reappeared late in the fifteenth century as an attempted fusion of the Middle Ages with classical antiquity. The Gothic style of France—as of England—which had developed with the growing life of the nation, and in which its highest aspirations had found expression, was firmly rooted, and, for some time at least, and at many points, the older tradition refused to be vanquished. There was in France, too, it must be remembered, no "Reformation" with its accompanying change of belief and of religious sentiment, and its disregard of ecclesiastical tradition. There was accordingly no cessation of church building, and no sudden change, for the needs of Catholic worship remained the same and were met in the old way, and a period of some length ensued during which the churches were still Gothic in their plan and general design, the old outlines being adhered to, and the new enthusiasm for classical art showing itself only in details. Thus, the spirit of the new fashion in architecture was still Gothic, but Gothic modified by the new forms of ornament which so delighted the men of the time, and this decoration was not conventional (like the early Gothic) or realistic (like the mid-Gothic) or natural (as the late Gothic had been), but fantastic. Men looked to Italy as the home of the arts, but they did not realise that architecture had never made Italy her chosen seat, and the "orders" of the ancients became the affectation of the time. The new movement brought no new inspiration with it, as it might have done if it had been truly what the name Renaissance implies; it had no life of its own to live, but appeared—in the first instance—as a parasite upon decaying Gothic, showing itself in parts of buildings such as porches (as at Le Grand-Andelys), façades (as at Villeneuve-sur-Yonne) or towers (as at St.-Thibault Joigny), or in accessories such as stalls, screens and organ-cases. As a mixed style in the fabric of the church this type of building began in France under Francis I, and lasted on until about the middle of the seventeenth century under Louis XIII, and very many noble churches exhibit the blend of classic detail with Gothic general conception.

It is instructive to compare the somewhat parallel course of the Renaissance movement in England. Early in the Tudor period the influence was Italian, as seen in the tomb of Henry VII at Westminster

(1512), in the Marney tomb at Layer Marney (Essex) and some other examples—or French as in the terra-cotta work in Wymondham and Oxborough churches (Norfolk). Then came the break of the Reformation, and in the reigns of Elizabeth and James I Renaissance additions to English churches were of a more clumsy type of design, showing the unmistakable influence of a Flemish school. Under the Laudian Anglo-Catholic revival churches were erected, as in France, of Gothic outline, with a veil of classic, as at St. Catherine Cree London or St. John's Leeds, but the "Jacobean" style was almost confined to houses for the nobility and gentry. In France, too, the early Renaissance was a time of great *château* building. Along the Loire valley, especially, mighty mansions arose. These were no longer grim fortresses of the feudal period, for France was emerging from the confusions of the Middle Ages and gaining her national unity, but the new art rapidly adapted itself to the conditions and the châteaux of the nobles, such as, Chenonceaux (1512–23), Chambord (1520–30) and many another in Touraine retained the high-sloping roofs, the towers, the extinguisher turrets and the spiral staircases of the Middle Ages.

As examples of the addition of Renaissance parts to earlier churches we may quote the following:

Châlons-sur-Marne Cathedral—the west façade.
St.-Alpin Châlons-sur-Marne—a doorway in the west front.
Rethel (Ardennes)—tower.
Villeneuve-sur-Yonne (Yonne)—the west façade.
St.-Pierre Saumur (Maine-et-Loire)—the façade.
St.-Léger Soissons—the façade and tower.
St.-Pierre Caen—the east end.
Ste.-Marie-du-Mont (Manche)—the tower.
Conches (Eure)—a doorway.
Le Grand-Andelys (Eure)—the north transept front.
Pierrefonds (Oise)—the tower.
Houdan (Seine-et-Oise)—the choir.

More or less complete churches frequently occur, and in a great many of these the classic features engrafted upon the Flamboyant are handled with a fineness of detail and a smallness of scale such as are not met with as a rule in Italian Renaissance. The style has a great deal of detail, yet so cleverly arranged that the structure does not appear overladen, and the resultant effect is often charming, as is undeniably the case at Gisors and Beaumont-le-Roger (Eure), Chaumont-en-Vexin (Oise), St.-Pierre Coutances (Manche), St.-Germain Argentan (Orne), Ste.-Trinité Falaise (Calvados), Vouziers (Ardennes), St.-Pierre Auxerre (Yonne), Auxon (Aube), St.-Calais (Sarthe), Rembercourt-aux-Pots (Meuse), St.-Michel Dijon, the façade of Notre-Dame-du-Marthuret Riom (Puy-de-Dôme) and the two Paris churches of St.-Eustache and St.-Étienne-du-Mont.

STE.-MARIE-DU-MONT (MANCHE).

W. NARTHEX-PORCH, ST.-PÈRE-SOUS-VÉZELAY (YONNE).

MID-GOTHIC.

facing p. 192.

Other examples which should be noted are the western towers and façade of Évreux Cathedral, the Cathedral at Blois, the façade of Luçon Cathedral, St.-Pantaléon Troyes and the church of Le-Ricey-Bas at Les Riceys (Aube), the Chapel of the Lycée at Chaumont (Hte.-Marne), Cravant (Yonne), St.-Pierre Douai (Nord), St.-Patrice Bayeux (Calvados), Vétheuil (Seine-et-Oise), St.-Rémi Dieppe, and the Chapel of the Sacred Heart at St.-Jacques in the same town, Notre-Dame Le Havre and the Chapel of the College at Eu (Seine-Inférieure): the last a very fine example in brick, with facings of the façade in stone.

In its details this early Renaissance style carried on the Gothic tradition, treating them in its own characteristic way.

Pillars are usually without capitals and are sometimes twisted or ornamented in a somewhat fantastic manner, as at Gisors (Eure). At St.-Germain Argentan, the piers in the choir aisle are formed of clusters of classical columns arranged in two tiers.

Vaults are in some cases treated with extravagance of ornament and a number of very elaborate and large pendants hang from the intersections of the ribs. Ornate and wonderful instances of the kind occur at Montfort-l'Amaury (Seine-et-Oise), St.-Germain Argentan, St.-Gervais Falaise and St.-Pierre Caen (Calvados) and, most fascinating of examples, the vaulting in the chancel and in the south chapel at the little village church of Tillières-sur-Avre (Eure).

The *fenestration* varies a good deal. Sometimes late Gothic forms of tracery are employed almost without change, save for the omission of cusping, as at Le-Ricey-Bas (Aube) and St.-Taurin Évreux, and in some windows of St.-Pierre Caen. In other cases the Renaissance sets out blithely to do Gothic work in the way of window tracery, with the result that we have such gay and fantastic forms as we meet with at Beaumont-le-Roger (Eure), where the monogram of the patron Saint, St. Nicholas, figures in the tracery in the head of a window. But not always is the result of attempts of the kind so pleasing, as witnesses the very odd endeavour to construct window tracery of classical forms at St.-Jean Troyes. Often the designers of this period fell back upon radiating tracery of fan-like form as at Notre-Dame Le Havre, the chapel of the Lycée at Chaumont (Hte.-Marne) and the head of a doorway at Conches (Eure). Altogether the problem of tracery seems to have presented considerable difficulty at this time owing to the prevalence of depressed segmental heads for the windows, and it is sometimes present only in a very tentative form, as at St.-Maurice Épinal (Vosges) or omitted altogether.

In *towers* there appeared the domical form of finish, which, according to Freeman, is the one point in which the Renaissance can compete with Gothic. This is seen in fine towers at St.-Germain Argentan, where the north-west tower is Gothic in conception, with pinnacles, flying buttresses and octagon lantern upon a massive square tower, but the pinnacles are urns and the octagon is covered by a shallow dome which carries a lantern for finish. Other examples of domical finish are found at Ste.-Marie-du-Mont (Manche), St.-Pierre Senlis (Oise), St.-Maclou and Notre-Dame Pontoise (Seine-et-Oise), Bressuire (Deux-Sèvres), the Cathedrals of Blois and Tours, Notre-Dame Bourg (Ain), the west towers of St. Michel Dijon and Asfeld (Ardennes).

The furnishing of churches within with such accessories as stalls, rood-screens, screens for chapels, organ-cases and pulpits, which marked the late Gothic period, also went on without interruption during the prevalence of this mixed style.

The *buffets-d'orgues* are so numerous throughout France that a list would be scarcely of value, and they are so uniformly splendid that it is impossible to single out representative examples for mention. One cannot

St.-Germain Argentan (Orne).

refrain, however, from noting the charming Renaissance organ-case at St.-Bertrand-de-Comminges (Hte.-Garonne) and the strange example at St.-Savin (Hte.-Garonne) with its row of demons' heads, whose eyes roll and whose tongues protrude, when the instrument is in action.

There are splendid examples of *choir stalls* in wood of which special reference may be made to those at

St.-Maximin (Var), Lescar (Basses-Pyrénées), St.-Germer (Oise), Valognes (Manche), the chapel of the château at Ussé (Indre-et-Loire), St.-Maixent (Deux-Sèvres), Bassac (Charente) Montbenoît (Doubs) and Montréal (Yonne).

Of *rood-screens* there are ornate and exquisitely finished instances in wood at St.-Bertrand-de-Comminges (Hte.-Garonne) and St.-Maximin (Var), and Brittany has wooden screens of intricate and delicate detail belonging to the sixteenth century at La-Roche-Maurice and the Chapel of St.-Herbot (Finistère), besides a splendid fragment at Ste.-Croix Quimperlé. The small rock-church of Haute-Isle on the Seine also contains a very good screen of Renaissance design. But more rood-screens of stone belonging to this period have come down to us. The remains of the Limoges Cathedral screen are now erected at the west end. At Appoigny (Yonne) and Arques-la-Bataille (Seine-Inférieure) are two beautiful ones *in situ*. St.-Étienne-du-Mont Paris has a large rood-screen of fantastic design with parapet of lace-like tracery, and approached by stone staircases that twine around the pillars on either side. St.-Géry Cambrai (Nord) and Notre-Dame-de-Liesse (Aisne) have screens of stone and marble, very grand and designed in the Flemish manner after the pattern of such screens as those of Tournai and Bruges Cathedrals. Delicate and well-designed screens to side-chapels are frequent as at St.-Jacques Dieppe, the Abbey of Fécamp (Seine-Inférieure), Notre-Dame St.-Omer (Pas-de-Calais) and the Cathedral of Laon.

Of *tombs* of the period those of the Cardinals of Amboise and of Louis de Brézè in the Lady Chapel of Rouen Cathedral are of extraordinary excellence, and equally remarkable is the monument of Thomas James at the Cathedral of Dol (Ille-et-Vilaine) of design quite foreign to Brittany and due to artists of a Florentine school.

Reredoses of this style abound. At Écouis (Eure) is a whole series of stalls with two reredoses, one on each side of the entrance to the choir, and in the one on the north a Madonna of exceptional beauty given by Francis I to this collegiate church. Some reredoses are of great beauty after the somewhat fanciful and exuberant fashion in vogue at the period, such as we may see in stone at St.-André-les-Vergers (Aube), Autun Cathedral and Hattonchâtel (Meuse), or in wood at St.-Wulfran Abbeville (Somme), Ligueil (Indre-et-Loire), the church of La Cité Périgueux, the Chapelle des Pénitents Gris at Aigues-Mortes (Gard) and the old Jesuits' Chapel at Arles. Many Renaissance altar-pieces in wood have twisted and wreathed pillars as a prominent feature of their design, as at the Lady Chapel of Rouen Cathedral, Pont-de-l'Arche (Eure), St. Martin Laigle (Orne), Ste.-Mère-Église (Manche) and the Chapelle of St.-Nicholas Compiègne (Oise). At Notre-Dame Calais a fine seventeenth-century reredos of Flemish type frames a good picture of the "Assumption," and the influence of Flemish style is seen in a beautiful reredos of the martyrdom of St.-Sebastian at Guiclan (Finistère).

At Brioude (Hte.-Loire) in the chapel of the Holy Cross is a *rétable* of unusually good design marked by dignity and restraint. In the extreme south-west at St.-Jean-de-Luz, Ciboure, Ainhoué and elsewhere the east end is treated in the adjacent Spanish manner, without a window over the altar, and having images in niches over the whole wall.

A notice of Renaissance furniture would not be complete without a reference to the very beautiful *baptistery* at Guimiliau (Finistère). This was erected in 1675, and is covered with carving characteristic of its date. It takes the form of an octagonal domical canopy over the font supported upon corkscrew pillars, and may be compared with Bishop Cosin's similar but loftier font-canopy at Durham Cathedral, dating from the same period. Analogous examples occur in the fifteenth-century Perpendicular canopies over the font in the Norfolk churches of Trunch, Bacton and St. Peter Mancroft Norwich.

Before passing on to the succeeding phase of Renaissance, reference must be made to a remarkable building that seems to stand rather in a class by itself. This is the imposing façade which remains from the Abbey church of St.-Amand-les-Eaux (Nord). The design has been attributed to Rubens. It bears the date 1633, and shows a tower in the centre with two flanking turrets all finished in domical form. The front below is treated so far as its broad outlines are concerned in the traditional French manner, with portal in the centre and a medallion of sculpture above, corresponding to the almost inevitable *rosaçe* of a French cathedral or abbey church. The whole scheme of ornament with which the façade is completely overlaid, even to the domes, is Spanish in its complexion, and lacks the daintiness of conception and delicacy of execution met with in early French Renaissance work.

(3) The Constructive Phase of Renaissance Style

The plaything which the men of the sixteenth century in France handled so gracefully and with such excellent effect was destined to grow into a tyrant. The iron hand of Vitruvius proved far-reaching, and the pleasing mixed style as seen in the churches just mentioned was succeeded, from Louis XIV to Louis XVI, by a frigid classicalism which dealt a death-blow to mystical art. The Renaissance style passed from its decorative and entered upon a constructive phase. Classic columns and pilasters were no longer superimposed upon a Gothic structure, but were themselves employed in construction.

As in England this period was largely an age of house-building. The enormous wealth of great families made possible the erection of châteaux vaster in scale, as also more numerous, than in England, before a terrible nemesis fell upon the nobles at the Revolution. During the seventeenth century fabulous sums were spent upon building by the Court and the State, but by degrees the church ceased to inspire design, and it is significant that at the beginning of the eighteenth century the chapel had disappeared from the plan of private mansions, or was reduced to the dimensions of a very small oratory, scarcely distinguishable in appearance from other rooms in the house.

Churches built at this time were more or less uniform throughout the land, and hence lacked that interest which arises from variety. There was now more unity than ever about the design of a church, for the Renaissance meant the complete abandonment of the older haphazard method of building such additions as need might require or fancy dictate. A great building was now from the first planned with balance and clearly conceived as a whole from the outset. This explains how it is that in Renaissance churches we miss the variety and the daintiness of the earlier Gothic to which it owes not a little of its charm, though it may be argued that there is some gain in restraint and distinction.

This style gave us the cold and severe Cathedrals of Arras, Cambrai, Rennes and La Rochelle, and such façades as those of the Cathedrals of Langres and Auch,

Étival (Vosges) and the church of St.-Christophe at Belfort (Haut-Rhin), in which the French tradition of two western towers proved too strong to be overcome. The Abbey of Mont-St.-Éloi (Pas-de-Calais), whose previously ruined façade was still further damaged in the Great War, was another example of the traditional type of west front carried out in heavy classical style.

Of churches on a smaller scale with more or less well-designed portico or pilastered front, many a provincial town affords an example. A number of these are without architectural interest, but pleasing instances of good and somewhat lofty proportion for their scale occur at Notre-Dame-de-la-Gloriette Caen (Calvados), St.-Vincent Blois (Loir-et-Cher), the church of the Visitation Le Mans (Sarthe), St.-Martin Troyes (Aube) and the Église-des-Minimes at Clermont-Ferrand (Puy-de-Dôme). The last has a well-designed small dome, and the examples at Blois, Le Mans and Troyes have domed belfries typical of the style.

Late classical churches can be poorly designed and bald in effect, as at St.-Georges Vesoul (Hte.-Saône), St.-Nicholas Boulogne (Pas-de-Calais) and St.-Louis Pau (Basses-Pyrénées), but in a few rare examples present fine decoration of *rococo* character, as in the interior of the Jesuits' church of Cambrai (Nord) with its strong suggestion of Spanish influence and the very dainty and beautifully planned façades of two small churches—the Chapel of the Visitation at Nevers and the Chapel of the Carmelites at Dijon.

Paris abounds in churches of the later Renaissance, such as St.-Roch (1650–1730) and St.-Sulpice (1650–1770), the latter a striking church sometimes referred to as the greatest effort of the Renaissance to outdo Gothic art. Its façade with two dissimilar towers is thoroughly in keeping with French tradition. It is in Paris, too, that we have grand examples of the *dome*, which was the finest contribution of the Renaissance to architecture in Western Europe. The four notable domed churches of the city are The Invalides, Ste.-Geneviève (the Panthéon), the Sorbonne and the Church of Val-de-Grâce. All four domes are of fine outline, and crowned by lanterns, while those of the Hôtel-des-Invalides (by Mansard, 1675–1706) and of the Panthéon (by Soufflot, 1757–84) are worthy to be classed with the domes of St. Peter's Rome, Florence Cathedral and St. Paul's London, as the most magnificent of the Renaissance domes of Europe.

The nineteenth-century church of the Madeleine in Paris is remarkable as having been designed altogether after the model of a temple in the Corinthian style, arranged internally as a Christian church, very impressively lighted from above, and with a large group of statuary placed for a reredos which is in keeping with its general design. Amongst the varied interest of the modern architecture of Paris, there are two other churches which especially claim attention—Ste.-Clothilde, a Mid-Gothic design with a pair of fine spires at the west front, and the great basilica of Sacré-Cœur at Montmartre, begun as a memorial to those who gave their lives in the war of 1870–1, and conceived in the domed style of Périgord, its central dome with four subsidiary cupolas, and its campanile, all calling to mind, in an external view, the outlines of the Cathedral of Périgueux.

Modern church architecture in France has proceeded, in general, upon traditional lines. The characteristic French Gothic type of church in which the principal feature is the western façade with its pair of towers has furnished the plan for such churches as Ste.-Clothilde Paris, Cholet (Maine-et-Loire), Notre-Dame-la-Délivrande (Calvados), St.-André Niort (Deux-Sèvres), Ste.-Baudille Nîmes and St.-Vincent-de-Paul Marseilles. But local variations of style have not always been thus over-ridden, and fine large churches have been erected at Périgueux in the manner of Périgord, and in the case of St.-Joseph at Clermont-Ferrand in the strongly marked Auvergnat type of Romanesque. Viollet-le-Duc, too, wisely completed the western towers of Clermont-Ferrand Cathedral in the dark volcanic stone of the district. At Le Havre again the church of St.-Vincent-de-Paul follows the three-towered plan of a Romanesque minster of Normandy. Modern facilities in construction have as yet led to no very notable departures in ecclesiastical architecture except in the two remarkable reinforced-concrete churches by Messrs. Perret at Le Raincy and Montmagny near Paris. Both churches are extraordinary feats in combining architectural quality with cheapness in construction. The plan of both churches is clean and simple, the method of framing on piers, with the walls as light infillings, being clearly visible, while the main effect of the interior is produced by large rectangular windows entirely filled with a network of geometrical tracery.

CHAPTER VIII

ON SOME SPECIAL CLASSES OF STRUCTURE

(1) Round or Polygonal Churches

At Neuvy-St.-Sépulcre (Indre) is the ancient round church from which the place is named: one of those copies of the church of the Holy Sepulchre at Jerusalem with which returning Crusaders dotted Western Europe.[1] This church at Neuvy is of outstanding interest, for the other great example in France at St.-Bénigne Dijon has become a mere crypt.[2] It is well known to archæology that the church built by Constantine over the grotto-tomb of Our Lord was a basilica with semi-circular apse. In the seventh century the Persian invaders of Palestine destroyed this building, and the Christians on restoring it did no more than complete the circle of the apse, so as to cover the Sacred Tomb in the centre, thus making a structure akin in plan to such mausoleum-churches as those of Hadrian in Rome (now known as the Castle of St.-Angelo) and of Theodoric in Ravenna. When the Crusaders came to Jerusalem they knew nothing of this architectural transformation, and so carried back with them to the West the plan of a round temple, which from that time stood in men's

[1] In England there are four round churches, all dedicated in the name of the Holy Sepulchre. They vary in date and style. Those at Cambridge and Northampton are Norman, the Temple Church London belongs to the Transition to Early English, and at Little Maplestead is a hexagonal arcade of the Decorated style. All four have naves added to the rotunda, like the example at Neuvy-St.-Sépulcre.

[2] On the round church at Lanleff in Brittany, see above, p. 119.

minds as the true image of the primitive church of the Holy Sepulchre. At Neuvy a late Romanesque nave was added in the thirteenth century to the original circular shrine. On the exterior the unbroken cylindrical wall of the rotunda has been surmounted by a second story with arcading, and the structure is covered by a small dome upon the inner drum of the upper gallery. The interior is most impressive with its circle of cylindrical columns, having finely carved deep capitals, and its altar in the centre where the Grotto of the Sepulchre was originally placed.

At Riez (Basses-Alpes) are many Roman remains and also a rotunda known as the Panthéon, with circumscribing aisle and a finely constructed octagonal dome supported by antique Corinthianesque pillars.

While in the West the basilica became the ordinary plan for a Christian church, in the Eastern Empire a centralised plan was used from an early date, in which the subsidiary parts were grouped round a central space. On this plan was developed the Byzantine style, of which the church of Sta.-Sophia at Constantinople stands as the great example. Owing to the current of Byzantine influence which flowed through south-western France, churches were built here and there on this centralised plan, so that we have circular or multangular naves with radiating apses. Three excellent examples remain. At Planès (Pyrénées-Orientales) is a small church of the thirteenth century triangular on the plan, with radiating apses, and becoming circular above. St.-Michel-sur-Charente (Charente) has an octagonal nave with radiating chapels of the twelfth century, and at Rieux-Minervois (Aude) is a round church of the eleventh century, whose original outline has been a good deal obscured by some later additions. A still earlier example of centralised plan is found amongst early Christian buildings grouped together at the Abbey of Mont-Majour near Arles (Bouches-du-Rhône). This is the Chapelle-Ste.-Croix attributed to Charlemagne, a small structure square on the plan with semi-circular apses opening out on each side.

Simpler still in plan is the small circular church of the eleventh century in the cemetery at Chambon (Puy-de-Dôme). This may have been built to serve as a mortuary chapel, though it is locally known as "the Baptistery."

Detached buildings erected for baptisteries have been mentioned above,[1] but at Le Puy, besides the Cathedral baptistery, there is another little detached building, octagonal on the plan, which stands near the foot of the needle-rock of St.-Michel. It is generally spoken of as the Temple of Diana and its purpose is not exactly known. Possibly it may have been erected as a mausoleum church, but it stands near the river and a fountain (the present structure of a later date) adjoins it, so that it is usual to class it with baptismal churches.

Montmorillon (Vienne) possesses two detached structures of some interest—one an octagonal building in the garden of the Seminary, whose purpose is not certainly known; the other a sepulchral chapel at the Maison Dieu. This latter dates from the twelfth century and is also octagonal in plan. Each side externally has a large shallow recessed pointed arch, and the stone roof rests upon a series of carved corbels. Unfortunately the building is incomplete and has lost the lantern which probably crowned it.

At St.-Émilion (Gironde) is a little building known as the "Rotonde." It is not really a circular building but a little apsidal chapel of transitional style. In the rock beneath is a small crypt with a spring of water.

[1] See p. 30 *n*.

This suggests that the structure belongs to the class of Well-Chapels, probably erected in the first instance to serve as baptisteries, of which there are examples in Cornwall at Dupath near Callington, St. Cleer near Liskeard and St. Breward near Bodmin.

Though it is much later in date than the buildings above noted, in this same class of detached structures we may place the very beautiful "Chapelle-des-Morts," or "Recevresse," as it is called, which stands just off the south transept of the church at Avioth (Meuse). This is hexagonal in plan and a perfect gem of early sixteenth-century Gothic. Its base is formed by cylindrical pillars which stand free, and above them rises a hexagonal screen of open tracery, niches and canopy-work surmounted by a crocketed spire which has pierced tracery between its ribs. The precise purpose for which this building was erected is not known. According to Viollet-le-Duc it was called "Chapelle-des-Morts" because the priest at the close of Mass, coming out from the church, would stand upon its platform to bid the prayers of the people for the dead. It seems to have gained also the name "La Recevresse" from the custom of placing within it, upon the Feast of the Patron Saint, offerings in kind of all sorts of produce of the district. In strong contrast to this dainty structure is the sepulchral chapel at Sarlat (Dordogne), a plain erection without any adornment, like a circular tower with stone finish of sugar-loaf shape.

(2) Bridge Chapels

In the Middle Ages there was no separation between religion and common life, so that works of public utility or for the benefit and convenience of travellers were considered as sacred works carried out under the sanction of religion and undertaken by religious orders or confraternities. The beneficent work of bridge-building was looked upon as especially sacred, as the associations of the word Pontiff remain to prove, and in accordance with its sacred character it was natural that a chapel should be erected in connection with a bridge, either resting upon one of its piers or built near the approach to it.[1]

The best known of these bridge-chapels in France is the one which stands on the second pile from the shore of the broken bridge of St.-Bénézet at Avignon. It is a little building of Romanesque style approached by a flight of steps that lead down from the roadway upon the bridge, and has a three-sided apse, taller than the rest of the chapel, upon the projecting pier. Facing the roadway is a bell gable with two openings. Tradition says that St.-Bénézet was a shepherd boy, who in the solitary hours of silent introspection that belong to a shepherd's life received a revelation from heaven that he must build a bridge across the Rhone. At any rate we know that he was one of the heads of the confraternity of "Hospitaliers pontifes" instituted in the twelfth century, whose special work it was to build bridges, to set up ferries and generally to assist travellers on the banks of rivers.

If the bridge-chapel at Avignon has been often visited and painted, the one at Pernes (Vaucluse) is probably almost unknown. Pernes is still partly enclosed by its ancient walls three of whose gates

[1] Bridge-chapels remain in England at Wakefield and Rotherham (Yorks), St. Ives (Hunts) and Bradford-on-Avon (Wilts). Quite another class of structure associated with bridges is a tower for their defence. The fortified bridges at Orthez (Basses-Pyrénées) and Sospel (Alpes-Maritimes) have a tower in the centre like the bridge over the Monnow at Monmouth in England. But the most splendid of all fortified bridges is the Pont-Valentré at Cahors with its three tall towers in line, one in the centre and one near either end.

remain. The Porte-Notre-Dame has its round flanking towers corbelled out from the walls and overhanging the little river Nesque, spanned immediately outside the gate by a bridge of two arches. Upon the middle pier is a tiny chapel with semi-circular apse and gable for one bell. The whole scene is most picturesque and romantic and seems unaltered since the Middle Ages.

At the approach to the old bridge at Carcassonne there stands on the right, as one goes from the lower town, a rectangular building of little architectural merit whose religious purpose is made evident by a Gothic window of two lights and a statue of Our Lady beneath a crocketed canopy upon the angle buttress. This little chapel is still in use, and over its entrance is written:

> Si l'amour de Marie
> En ton cœur est gravé
> En passant ne l'oubliez
> Viens lui dire un Ave.

(3) Fortified Churches

From what has been said above as to the lack of national unity in France during the Middle Ages, and its slow growth amid much internecine strife between counties, provinces and kingdoms, it will readily be gathered that there was much need for the strengthening of buildings of all kinds, that they might be the better able to resist attack. We find, accordingly, that there are a good many examples of fortified churches, especially near the coast, and upon a frontier, such as the Pyrénées district, liable to constant raids, forays and disturbances.[1]

[1] The sea-coast and a land frontier are the usual quarters in which we may expect to find fortified churches. In Britain they occur e.g. near the Scottish border, as at Great Salkeld (Cumberland) and Ancroft (Northumberland), and in South Wales, where the typical native churches

S. FAÇADE, LOUVIERS (EURE).

ROOD-SCREEN, LA MADELEINE TROYES.

FLAMBOYANT.

facing p. 208.

(A) The most important churches of this class are those which were *built wholly as fortified structures*, and there are several most interesting examples of the kind.

At Royat (Puy-de-Dôme) is the fortified church of a community of Benedictine nuns in a romantic situation amongst the Auvergnat volcanoes. It is an aisleless cruciform church of the simplest kind, without chapels and having a rectangular east end. The walls are square and lofty without projections save the flat buttresses which help to carry the elaborate system of machicolation. It has a narthex probably once crowned, like other Auvergnat churches, by a western tower. The present central octagon is modern, for pictures drawn in the earlier half of the last century show the church without it.

The Mediterranean coast has three fine specimens of fortress-church. Those at Agde (Hérault) and Les-Saintes-Maries (Bouches-du-Rhône) are massive rectangular structures battlemented throughout and with deeply recessed external arcading for machicolation carried by a range of pilaster-like buttresses. At Agde there is a square fortified tower, but the church of Les-Saintes-Maries is towerless, the battlemented shrine of the patron saints being raised high above the semi-circular apse in tower-like fashion, and this again carries a triple gable with openings for bells in two tiers. The other Mediterranean fortress-church is the Abbey of St.-Victor at Marseilles, a building enclosed by an almost blank wall like a castle, battlemented and with rectangular battlemented towers, large rectangular battlemented turrets being disposed round the apse like huge deep buttresses. In these churches the

are towerless, we have a long line of massive church towers, evidently intended for purposes of refuge or defence along the shores of the Bristol Channel and of Cardigan Bay.

windows are very few and reduced to dimensions as small as possible.

Luz-St.-Sauveur (Htes.-Pyrénées) has a practically unaltered, though restored, church of the Templars, very strongly fortified and having a massive battlemented *enceinte*, with machicolated entrance tower. The church itself is aisleless with apse, and its windows are small and very high up in the wall, just beneath a low-pitched roof. In the defences of this remarkable church are *hourdes*—wooden galleries resting upon bold corbels in the wall, from the shelter of which archers might repel an attack without much danger to themselves.

At Esnandes (Charente-Inférieure) on the Biscay coast is a remarkable fortified church. It is a rectangular building, battlemented throughout, with its western portion elevated into a sort of castle with heavy and far-projecting battlemented machicolation.

Another complete fortified church exists at Le Boupère (Vendée). It is almost windowless and the side walls are machicolated. The west front is flanked by circular fortress turrets between which runs a machicolated gallery at the top of the façade.

But most picturesque of all instances of a church militant in a very literal sense is the one at Simorre (Gers)—a veritable fortress of the fourteenth and fifteenth centuries, constructed in brick. The whole building, as well as the tower, is battlemented, and its boldly projecting buttresses with pyramidal caps are as bastions in a castle wall.

(B) A good many churches, planned after the usual fashion for a church, and whose whole appearance is not affected by military considerations, are yet *fortified in some particular part.*

The apse at Vénerque (Hte.-Garonne) has its walls

carried up and battlemented, so that it has the appearance of a fortified tower. At Le Dorat (Haute-Vienne), the easternmost of the radiating chapels is carried up to a great height and machicolated, so that in a general view it has the appearance of a slender tower at the extreme east end of the church, in line with the tall central octagon and the massive square

Simorre (Gers) Brick Fortified Church.

narthex tower at the west.[1] The church of St.-Paulien (Hte.-Loire) has a remarkable east end also. In this case the church is terminated towards the east by two large apses, unbuttressed and windowless, like two great bastions of a fortress.

[1] The exterior of this church presents a remarkable outline, for in addition to the three axial towers referred to, there are four subsidiary Romanesque turrets of open arches with short spires. Two of these flank the western tower at the façade, while the other two are set on either side of the choir.

At Brioude (Hte.-Loire) the transept ends have high up on their external face a wide arch extending nearly from angle to angle. These arches stand out in front of and apart from the wall, and serve the purpose of machicolations, being obviously constructed as a defensive work.

There are somewhat similar arches with machicola-

LE DORAT (HAUTE-VIENNE).

tions along the front of the curious chapel on the north side of the choir at Redon (Ille-et-Vilaine).

At Écoyeux (Charente-Inférieure) the west front is flanked by machicolated turrets, while at Lodève (Hérault), in addition to flanking turrets, a machicolated gallery runs across the top of the façade. The little church of St.-Pierre-de-Rhèdes in the same Department is similarly protected at its west end. Again, at the west end of Quintenas (Ardèche) and Authon (Charente) are battlements and machicolations, while St.-Jacques

Montauban and Caussade (Tarn-et-Garonne) have machicolations high up in the façade. The last two churches belong to the brick type of architecture, which characterises the whole district of the Tarn and about Toulouse, and some churches of the locality are strongly fortified, those at Rabastens (Tarn) and Montesquieu-Volvestre (Hte.-Garonne), for example, having for their western façades huge blank fortress walls with very small openings.

Farther north on the banks of the Loire the west ends of the churches of Cunault (Maine-et-Loire) and Candes (Indre-et-Loire) are heavily battlemented, and at Candes the battlement is also carried round the upper part of the very beautiful and singular north porch.

Fortified towers occur here and there,[1] as at Albi Cathedral, Houcillès (Lot-et-Garonne), Villeneuve-lès-Avignon (Gard) and St.-Maurice (Vienne). The last is a central tower, without any lights, and has a curious bastion-like projection corbelled out at each angle. In the district about Toulouse where the belfry takes the *clocher-mur*, or screen, form characteristic of the neighbourhood, it is often strongly fortified, as at Gaillac-Toulza, Villenouvelle, Mourville-Hautes, Pont-charramet and Montgiscard (Hte.-Garonne). The screen-belfry at the west end of the Chapel of Notre-Dame-de-Sabart at Tarascon-sur-Ariège (Ariège) is both battlemented and machicolated, and other examples of fortified Pyrénéan belfries occur at St.-Girons and Montjoie (Ariège), the last a lofty example with a triplet of turrets.

At Druyes (Yonne) the west front is flanked on its southern side by a round machicolated tower, and at Uzerche (Corrèze) is another massive round tower,

[1] On some peculiarities of towers in Brittany, see above, p. 120.

adjoining in the church in the like position, loopholed and without ornament or windows.

(C) In other cases *the presence of a battlement* indicates the intention to fortify a church, for the use of the battlement, which is properly a feature of military architecture, as an ornamental finish or cresting, is confined in ecclesiastical architecture to England. In France it only appears in fortified churches,[1] with its proper object in view, and battlements occur:

In towers, as at Elne, St.-Michel-de-Cuxa, Serdynia and St.-Martin-du-Canigou Casteil (Pyrénées-Orientales), St.-Lizier-de-Couserans and St.-Girons (Ariège), Clermont-l'Hérault (Hérault), Entrevaux (Basses-Alpes) and Tayac (Dordogne).

On flying arches round the apse and turrets on the towers of Narbonne Cathedral (Aude).

On the apse at Fréjus (Var) and on a desecrated church at Narbonne, now used as a museum.

On the west screen-tower at St.-Nazaire Carcassonne, and the Église-du-Taur Toulouse.

On turrets of the portal at the Cathedral of Albi.

On the Biscay coast the battlement appears at Courçon (Charente-Inférieure), and on the Calvados coast at Luc-sur-Mer and Hermanville.

In the north fortified churches occur in the Department of Pas-de-Calais at Cremarest and Lottinghem. The second was used as a fort against the incursions of the Spaniards. It is loopholed, and the chimney that was used for cooking by those besieged within it may still be seen. The church tower of Dannes has two stone chimneys indicating the like purpose. At Le Crotoy (Somme) the modern church retains an ancient fortified tower. But the most interesting example in this part of France of fortification in connection with a church is

[1] The only example of a battlement in a French church as a purely ornamental feature appears to be in the tower of St.-Jacques Dieppe, and in that case it is treated as a band of pierced ornament in the French manner occurring below the belfry stage.

at Notre-Dame Calais. This church lies behind a grim protecting wall on its northern side, and the north transept front is flanked by two massive circular turrets battlemented at the top.

(4) Rock Churches

Dwellings hewn out of the rock are not uncommon in some parts of France. We meet with them in the valleys of the Cher and Indre, and they are fairly common in the neighbourhood of Loches (Indre-et-Loire) and in the district about Château-du-Loir (Sarthe). In view of this it is not surprising that there should be some examples of rock churches. In the valley of the Seine, there is a church hewn out in the side of the chalk cliff at La-Haute-Isle near La-Roche-Guyon above Vernon. It is a single chamber within, lighted by a range of five round-headed apertures in which window-frames are set, and above there crops up picturesquely from the rock a little square belfry. Altogether more imposing and on a much greater scale is the rock church of St.-Émilion assigned to a date as early as the ninth century. The scene outside the church is very striking. There are fragments of ancient walls and towers, and near by the little building known as "La Rotonde"[1]; then, against the abrupt face of the cliff behind which the church has been hollowed out, is a fourteenth-century Gothic portal with double doorway. On the level platform of rock above there rises a tall Gothic tower with crocketed spire. Within, the church consists of nave and aisles, separated by immense square piers that have been left in the solid rock. The roof has been hollowed out like a tunnel and the round arches of the arcade run into its curved surface. In its effect the church is

[1] See above, p. 205.

altogether unlike a Christian sanctuary of the West, and rather suggests a comparison with cave-temples in lands of the far distant East. The churches of Haute-Isle and St.-Émilion, with the curious church of St.-Jean at Aubeterre (Charente), form the three examples in France of Christian rock-sanctuaries.

(5) Cloisters

It is, perhaps, scarcely realised in how many instances cloisters or covered walks remain in France attached to cathedrals, or churches that were formerly of cathedral rank, to collegiate churches and to monasteries. A classified list of these, with some short notes, may be useful for reference and is here appended.

(*A*) *Romanesque Cloisters*

A type of the eleventh and twelfth centuries has double columns with elaborately carved capitals bearing semi-circular arches. Splendid cloisters of this kind are at Elne (Pyrénées-Orientales), where the shafts are very ornate, being diapered, twisted or chamfered to octagonal form—St.-Lizier-de-Couserans (Ariège), St.-Bertrand-de-Comminges (Hte.-Garonne), Vaison-La-Romaine (Vaucluse), Aix, St.-Rémy, Mont-Majour and St.-Trophime Arles (Bouches-du-Rhône). At Moissac (Tarn-et-Garonne) and in the Cloitre de Flaran Valence-sur-Baïse (Gers) coupled pillars of like character support pointed arches in the arcade dating from the twelfth century.

Other good examples of Romanesque cloisters occur at Ardelay (with coupled shafts and fine capitals) and Nieul-sur-l'Autize (Vendée), St.-Aubin Angers, Périgueux Cathedral, Fontfroide (Aude) and Lavadieu (Hte.-Loire).

At Le Puy Cathedral the outer face of the cloister

is adorned with flush-work patterns characteristic of the Auvergnat churches. St.-Donat (Drôme) has a curious example with an upper gallery, the arches of which are trefoiled. At Vannes (Morbihan) are some remains of a cloister with heavy cylindrical columns, and Daoulas (Finistère) has more extensive remains of a Romanesque cloister with coupled columns. The interesting ruins of the early monastery of Lerins on the Ile-St.-Honorat (Alpes-Maritimes) include a small cloister court with pointed arches and slender columns dating from the eleventh century.

Of a rather different kind is the covered walk with Romanesque arcade that runs along the south side of the church at Marmande (Lot-et-Garonne), in a manner that reminds one of the external stone galleries or cloisters of churches in Spain, such as San Vicente Avila, San Miguel de Escalada Léon, and at Segovia in the churches of San Martin, San Esteban, San Lorenzo and San Millan.

(B) Early Gothic

At St.-Émilion (Gironde) the cloister has plain pointed arches. Le Bourget (Savoie) and Arles-sur-Tech (Pyrénées-Orientales) have simple arcades of early pointed style, the latter retaining the double shafts characteristic of early Romanesque examples. Good cloisters of the thirteenth century remain at Fréjus and St.-Maximin (Var), Villefranche-de-Rouergue (Aveyron)—very graceful and with an interesting lavabo—and at Langres Cathedral (Hte.-Marne). Noyon Cathedral (Oise) has also an early Gothic cloister.

The splendid cloister-court at Mont-St.-Michel is exceptional in its design, having a double arcade in which the pillars of the outer range are set in front of the arches of the rear arcade. The details are "Early

English," the capitals being simply moulded and having the round abacus belonging to Anglo-Norman work of the early Gothic style, while the carved conventional foliage in the spandrels between the arches is akin to English work.

(*C*) *Mid-Gothic*

Of the period of Mid-Gothic there are some very splendid examples belonging to the fourteenth century, whose bays are filled in with characteristic tracery of the style, as at Larroumieu (Gers), St.-Hilaire and St.-Papoul (Aude), Chanteuges and La-Chaise-Dieu (Hte.-Loire), Bayonne Cathedral, Noirlac (Cher), St.-Dié (Vosges), the Dominican cloister at Colmar (Haut-Rhin)—now a museum—and St.-Jean-de-Vignes Soissons (Aisne). The cloister at Soissons must have been of exceptional beauty, but is sadly mutilated, most of the tracery having been broken away. The example at St.-Dié is remarkable for its exterior stone pulpit. This is not a common feature in France. There is, however, a graceful one of Flamboyant design at Notre-Dame St.-Lô (Manche) and another at Vitré (Ille-et-Vilaine). The preaching-cross at Pleubian (Côtes-du-Nord) has a fifteenth-century stone pulpit with figure sculpture, attached to its base, and a later Renaissance one of plain and heavy design projects from the church wall at Guerno (Finistère).

Of the fourteenth century also is the curious cloister of the Augustins at Toulouse (now a museum). The whole of the walks remain with coupled shafts and sculptured capitals, but above these, in place of the simple pointed arcade they must have been designed to bear, is a range of late Gothic tracery. Its cusped openings are pierced in thin stones, which are not thick enough to reach nearly across the double capitals.

To the same period belongs most of the cloister at Charlieu (Loire), though some part of it is Romanesque.

(*D*) *Late Gothic*

Cloisters of the later or Flamboyant Gothic are not so common as might be expected, but there are some fine examples, in most cases having characteristic unglazed tracery, as at the Cordeliers St.-Émilion (Gironde) of the fifteenth century. The cloister at Ambronay (Ain) has very good tracery, and an upper gallery or open loggia of wood of later date that is reached by a fine Renaissance staircase. Of the same period are the cloisters at Cahors Cathedral, Luxeuil-les-Bains (Hte.-Savoie), Montbenoît (Doubs), St.-Jean-de-Maurienne (Savoie) and Tréguier (Côtes-du-Nord). Other good cloisters are found at Tulle Cathedral, Cadouin (Dordogne), St.-Nazaire Béziers (Hérault), Verdun Cathedral (Meuse), St.-Gengoult Toul (Meurthe-et-Moselle) and St.-Wandrille-sur-Rançon (Seine-Inférieure). Of later sixteenth-century Gothic is the cloister at Brou (Ain).

(*E*) *Renaissance*

Cloisters of this style were designed in plain and heavy fashion. A few examples are worthy of mention, such as those of the Abbey of Fontevrault (Maine-et-Loire), St.-Germain Auxerre and a range of the cloister of the Carmelites at Gisors attached to a building that now serves for the Hôtel-de-Ville.

(*F*) *Wooden Cloisters*

A wooden cloister remains at the Convent of the Capuchins at Évreux, of the seventeenth century, and there is a most picturesque wooden gallery of the sixteenth century at St.-Maclou Rouen, running round the ancient burying-ground and known as the *aitre* St.-Maclou. A very similar example is found also at the cemetery of Brise-Garet, Montivilliers (Seine-Inférieure). The external cloister of wood at Bar-sur-Aube has been already referred to.[1] A most famous and beautiful instance of this class of structure is in the courtyard of the Hospital at Beaune (Côte-d'Or).

(6) Brick Churches

The first three sections of this chapter were concerned with churches whose particular form or features were determined by the purpose which the builders had in view. When we passed on to consider rock-churches we were dealing with structures whose form, or perhaps we should say whose lack of form, is due to an accident of geological conditions. Now all through the greater part of France there is abundant supply of good building stone—granite in Brittany—a fact which goes a long way to account for the French having always been a building people, and for the general prevalence of churches vaulted in stone, and this not only in the case of cathedrals, abbeys and collegiate churches, but in parish churches also both of towns and villages. In this respect there is a remarkable contrast between French and English churches, for in England there are no vaulted parochial churches, the stone vault being only used in subsidiary parts of the building such as the chancel, or transept, or perhaps a side chapel,[2] while even the greater churches in some cases have their nave covered by a wooden roof, as at Peterborough Cathedral and Southwell Minster.

[1] See above, p. 15. The only parallel to this in England is at Lurgashall (Sussex), where there is a covered walk on the south side of the nave, now closed in and used as a vestry.

[2] See *Parish Church Architecture*, pp. 100, 129, 144.

There are, however, districts in France where good building stone is obtainable with difficulty, and the church builders accordingly fell back upon the use of the artificial material of brick. The two districts that are in this way characterised by a prevalence of brick churches are a fairly wide region of the south-west of which Toulouse is the centre, and the northern departments corresponding to old French Flanders, where the character of the country, the race of the people, and the complexion of the architecture are alike allied to what we find in these respects upon the other side of the Belgian border. Something must here be said of the architecture of each of these districts in turn.

(A) The Brick Architecture of the South-West

In the city of Toulouse the prevailing material of the churches is brick, the bricks employed being large and thin as though derived in their form from the old Roman city of Tolosa, and their warm red colour has earned for the place the name of "la Ville Rose." The greatest of all the churches of Toulouse is St.-Sernin, consecrated in 1090, and therefore in building at the same time as the "Norman" Cathedral of Rochester and the Abbey of St. Albans in England. The exterior is almost all of brick, the transepts being in horizontal courses of brick and stone, and the doorways in stone. Its internal effect is very impressive by its narrow spacing, massive piers with plain square-edged arches placed close together, and cavern-like vault rendered dim through the absence of clerestory.

The tall brick tower and spire of Notre-Dame-de-la-Dalbade (sixteenth century) figures prominently in a general view of the city, the pediment of its battlemented west front being crowned also by three bold pinnacles, circular in shape and constructed, like the whole of the church, in brick. Within, the wide span of the nave and large wide apse have fine effect.

Of the other brick churches of the city the Église-du-Taur is of singular plan, an aisleless nave terminating eastwards in two apses, side by side, with a window high up in the wall between them.

The very large church of the Jacobines is an example of Hall-church,[1] its plan being formed by the juxtaposition, as it were, of two parallel naves, so that the range of immensely tall cylindrical pillars stretches along the centre of the interior up to the quadripartite vault, the ribs of the seven-sided apse springing from the easternmost pillar with wonderful effect.

Another church all of brick is the small one of St.-Jerome. Its planning is curious, though difficult to make out, as it is masked by houses, but it is of two bays with strongly convex walls externally, and a small octagonal bell-tower, also of brick, in the recess between them.

Apart from the city of Toulouse the greatest of the brick churches of the south is the Cathedral of Albi. Upon this strange church very varied opinions have been expressed. Its exterior, which rather suggests King's Chapel Cambridge, with the west tower of Ely Cathedral joined on to it, has not found favour with critics. It has been said that it despises beauty, and it has been compared to an animal monstrosity, as though some strange pink hairless and uncouth creature had crawled up from the deep cleft of the river Tarn and lay basking upon its bank. The whole church is like a castle, the west tower having huge circular angle buttresses in its lower part, and the expanse of the aisleless walls being broken by a long range of closely

[1] See p. 57.

placed bastion-like buttresses that reach up to the skyline.

This great cathedral, finished towards the end of the fifteenth century, is all of brick except the window tracery and the south porch, which seems to bear traces of Spanish influence. The interior is a vast unbroken hall, without aisles or pillars, of twelve bays with a five-sided apse at the east, and suggests the Angevin conception of a nave translated into terms of Gothic style. The outer walls are set towards the outer edge of the large lateral buttresses, so that the windows are scarcely seen in a general view of the interior. This method of lighting is most artistic, and it combines with the rich colouring of walls and vault, and with the sense of spaciousness, to produce an interior which must surely be ranked amongst the most impressive in the world. A ritual choir with ambulatory is formed by carved screen work and stalls of Flamboyant character and of the most marvellous delicacy and refinement. A similar arrangement is found at Condom (Gers), where a ritual choir and ambulatory is also formed by a fine screen of late Gothic design, but without the rood-screen at its entrance which we have at Albi.

All along the banks of the Tarn brick towns are precariously piled, and amongst them Rabastens on its exceptionally picturesque site is remarkable for a curious brick church whose tower, like that of Albi Cathedral, was evidently built with a military purpose in view. The church is clothed within, as with a dim richly-woven tissue, by (restored) fourteenth century frescoes.

In this region of brick building the design of belfries seems to be affected in two ways. Many towers are octagonal as at St.-Sernin Toulouse, the towers of the Jacobines and Augustins in the same city, with the very similar tall tower at Lombez (Gers), Notre-Dame

Millau (Aveyron), Grenade, St.-Félix-de-Caraman and L'isle-d'Albi (Tarn), St.-Jacques Montauban, Rieux, Beaumont-de-Lomagne and Caussade (Tarn-et-Garonne), and Pamiers and St.-Lizier-de-Couserans (Ariège), while some square towers have an octagonal story superimposed, as at Albi Cathedral and Notre-Dame-de-la-Dalbade Toulouse. But often the belfry takes, in this locality, the form of a high brick screen-front or wall in which openings are pierced for the bells. A grand example of this style is raised above the west front of the Église-du-Taur at Toulouse, and other instances occur at Montgiscard and Villefranche (with two tiers of arches), Gaillac-Toulza, Caignac, Villenouvelle, Pibrac and Baziège (with three tiers) (Hte.-Garonne), in each case flanked by turrets.

St.-Jacques Montauban.

ST.-PIERRE AUXERRE.

CHAPEL OF THE VISITATION, NEVERS.

RENAISSANCE.

facing p. 224.

In both types of belfry, whether screen or tower, the arches of openings and arcading commonly take the straight-sided or triangular-headed form which is a strongly marked characteristic of the brick architecture

VILLENOUVELLE (HAUTE-GARONNE).

of the district,[1] and where two lights are coupled together a lozenge-shaped opening is often inserted above them, the whole group being enclosed in a larger straight-sided arch. Typical instances occur in the upper stages of the towers of St.-Sernin Toulouse and Albi Cathedral,

[1] This form of arch, executed in Roman bricks similar in kind to those in use at Toulouse, occurs in the west doorway of Holy Trinity Colchester in England.

and at the Église-du-Taur Toulouse, the towers of the Jacobines and Augustins in the same city, Lombez (Gers), L'isle-d'Albi (Tarn), St.-Lizier-de-Couserans (Ariège) and St.-Jacques Montauban, with the other octagonal brick towers mentioned in the preceding paragraph.

(*B*) *The Brick Architecture of the North*

Many of the brick churches in the north are small, late in date and of little or no architectural interest, but several are of interest and worthy of remark. Tilloloy (Somme) has a charming church of well-executed brickwork. It is cruciform in plan and of late Gothic design (sixteenth century) with some classical detail. Its west front is in form like a château, with round flanking towers covered by slated extinguisher caps. Above the doorway runs a gallery with pierced parapet, and above this again a *rosaçe*, the whole terminated by a finely-crocketed gable. Hesdin and St.-Pol (Pas-de-Calais) have good brick churches with well-designed façades of Flemish type, that of St. Pol having three gables stepped in the manner characteristic of the Low Countries. St.-Waast Béthune (Pas-de-Calais) is a larger church of late Gothic, of the type one finds on the Franco-Belgian border, with tall slender columns bearing an elaborate vault of the *lierne* type. The church has neither triforium nor clerestory, and at its west end rises a nobly designed square tower. St.-Waast at Bailleul (Nord) is another brick church with massive square tower. It has three avenues separately gabled so that there is neither triforium nor clerestory, and the interior has been thoroughly classicalised. The church of St.-Pierre at Aire-sur-la-Lys (Pas-de-Calais) is an imposing building more in French style than those just referred to, and in its windows has good stone geometrical tracery.

At Hazebrouck (Nord) is a good brick tower. Notre-Dame Calais is a complete cruciform church with central tower all of brick. Its tower is of very decided Flemish character bearing a strong family likeness to those of Courtemarck, Merckem and Enghien across the Belgian border, but the rest of the church is quite English in some of its details. There is "Perpendicular" tracery in some of its windows, and the large window of the north transept is thoroughly "Perpendicular," its head enclosed in a square form, and the spandrels filled in with blank tracery. The detail and the general effect are here quite English, and we are not surprised to find them so, seeing that Calais was in English hands from the French wars of Edward III until the Duc-de-Guise recaptured it in the reign of the English Queen Mary.

(7) Wooden Churches

In view of what has been said above as to the abundance of good stone in France generally, it is not surprising that there is little use of wood in the structure of churches. It is in Normandy chiefly that wood is employed to any large extent for building purposes. In the villages there are many wooden houses, and farm buildings are commonly constructed of half-timbered work. In the towns, too, there are sometimes whole streets of most picturesque wooden houses, as at Lisieux (Calvados) and Caudebec-en-Caux (Seine-Inférieure), that have furnished many a subject for artists.

It is, accordingly, in this part of France that we find woodwork in portions of churches more often than elsewhere. The usual belfry for village churches over a large part of the Departments of Calvados, Eure and Seine-Inférieure is a small square tower upon the west gable, or upon the roof-ridge, with *flèche*, all constructed in wood and covered with slates, shingles, or occasionally leaded.

The smaller churches also sometimes have porches of wood. There is a good one of this material at the west end of Auvillars (Calvados). The church at Rocques (Calvados) has two wooden porches, one lateral and one western, and at Norolles and Fauguernon (Calvados) are larger wooden porches stretching across the west end of the church forming a sort of cloister, a feature occurring also at Cheverney (Loir-et-Cher) and Nohant (Indre).[1] The church of Pinterville (Eure) may be referred to as showing the use of wood in its parts, like so many Normandy villages, and very pleasing is its *tout ensemble* as viewed from the south side. It is an aisleless church and between the nave and chancel there rises from the roof a small square wooden belfry with shingled spire. Nearly in the centre of the nave is a polygonal porch of flat open arches of wood, and a short distance eastward from this there also projects from the nave a turret, semi-octagonal in form, and of stone up to the level of the eaves of the roof, but above is a half-timbered story finished with a pointed roof.

Ste.-Catherine at Honfleur (Calvados) furnishes a large complete example of the use of wood in church building, and it is all of wood, including even its detached tower and spire. The tower stands apart in the market-place, opposite the west front of the church. It has a square base, partly of stone and partly of half-timbered work, and from within this, rising out of its tiled roof, springs the square tower with octagonal spire of wavy outline. The structure leans a little and is shored up by long timber props stretching, like flying buttresses, from the angles of the tower to the roof of its base. The building as a whole dates from the close of the fifteenth century, but a classical portico of rather poor

[1] In England the little church at Leigh (Surrey) has a somewhat similar cloister-porch occupying the whole of the lower part of the west end.

Roman Doric design has been added at the west end. This last is now in process of demolition (1927), and a

PINTERVILLE (EURE).

scheme for the west front showing its timber construction is to be carried out. The plan of the church is curious, consisting of two naves in juxtaposition, each with a large apse at the east, and beyond this double body an aisle on either side. There is thus a row of wooden pillars down the centre of the interior, and other shorter ones separate the naves from their aisles. The coved timber roof is pointed, and has tie-beams and struts from below from the central pillars and from the

STE.-CATHÉRINE HONFLEUR (CALVADOS).

sides. The windows everywhere, in aisles and clerestory, and also the larger ones in the three-sided apses, are square-headed, as is most suitable in a structure of the kind. A similar wooden steeple to that of Ste.-Catherine is also found at the smaller church of St.-Étienne Honfleur (now a museum), and the same church has a good example of verandah-porch across its façade. Allouville-Bellefosse (Seine-Inférieure) has a curiosity in its sacred oak, within whose trunk are two small chapels, one above another, protected by a casing of oak shingles.

Of other parts of France, the Department of Aube is noted for good woodwork. The fine cloister-porch of Bar-sur-Aube has been already referred to. The church of Villemaur in the same Department has a very remarkable belfry of wood, in the form of five superimposed pyramids, a structure of the same class as the tower at Brookland (Kent). The village churches of the district often have half-timbered work in the upper part of the nave walls, as at Écriennes (Marne), or in the clerestory where there are aisles as at Favresse (Marne), but many of these churches suffered severely in the Great War.

(8) Town Belfries

We commonly call up visions of places by the towers that stand out from the surrounding buildings. The name of Salisbury will at once suggest its slender spire. Coventry must always be associated with the three tall spires commemorated in Tennyson's verse. Venice can scarcely be thought of apart from a vision of the tall companile of San Marco, and the mention of Bruges at once brings to mind its famous belfry that made such strong appeal to Longfellow's imagination. Generally it is the massive tower or graceful spire of a cathedral or parochial church that thus seems to sum up the impression of a place, but in northern France, as in Flanders generally, the specially significant structures that embody the *genius loci* are the remarkable Town Belfries, the outward and visible signs of the freedom, the power and the prosperity of the great free-trading communities amongst which Bruges and Ghent took foremost place.

The period from the eleventh to the fourteenth century was marked by a long struggle on the part of the communes to exercise without prejudice the rights which had been conferred upon them in charters, and to win for themselves independence of the despotic authority of the feudal lords. The building of a town hall was the earliest symbol of the growth of the free community, and the cities of Bordeaux and Toulouse had each a building of the kind as far back as the twelfth century. In the early days of enfranchisement it was customary to call together the citizens of the community by means of bells. These were, however, at first confined to the towers of churches, and since they could not be rung without the consent of the clergy a good deal of friction must sometimes have arisen, especially in those places where it happened that ecclesiastics were the feudal lords. To obviate difficulty of this kind the municipalities began to procure bells of their own, and these were hung at first over the town gates, in the manner of which an interesting example may still be seen in the gate known as La-Grosse-Cloche at Bordeaux.

Towards the close of the twelfth century and in the early years of the thirteenth we find that separate towers began to be erected for the town bells. Such towers also served the purpose of look-out, being provided with a lodging for the watchman and a gallery commanding a view on every side, so that the bell might sound an alarm upon outbreak of fire, or onset of a foe. While in their origin the belfries were thus designed to meet a need and serve a utilitarian purpose, they came to be regarded, as time went on, as ends in themselves, and were built on a great scale and lavishly adorned. This was especially the case in the north, where they were considered as ornamental features reared for their own sake, and such as no town of any pretension could be without. Thus the Town Belfries which form so regular a feature of old Flemish cities, and which occur with like frequency in northern France, may be looked upon as material symbols of the power and wealth of the communities that erected them.

The design and position of these town belfries vary a good deal. It was a reminiscence of early custom that led the builders to erect their belfry either above the town gate, as at Vire (Calvados), Amboise (Indre-et-Loire), Déols (Indre), Méhun-sur-Yevre and Vierzon (Cher), Avallon (Yonne) and Besse-en-Chandesse (Puy-de-Dôme), or adjoining it as at Auxerre and in the example of La-Grosse-Horloge at Rouen. Very frequently in Flanders, whether in Belgium or in Northern France, the bell-tower forms a part—often the central feature—of the Hôtel-de-Ville or other important building belonging to the municipality, as at Bruges, Bergues (Nord), Calais and Hesdin (Pas-de-Calais), Rue and Abbeville (Somme), and in the splendid examples at Ypres and Arras which perished in the Great War. But in some cases the bell-tower was a detached and isolated building, as at Ghent and Tournai in Belgium, and at Amiens and St.-Ricquier (Somme) and Évreux (Eure). At Béthune (Pas-de-Calais) and Moulins (Allier) the belfries are not attached to a public building but have dwelling-houses erected around them.

The belfries differ a good deal, too, in the character of their architecture. Those above gates have slated spires or pointed roofs, as at Bordeaux and Besse-en-Chandesse. Some of the earlier ones, having been built in the troubled days of the growing communes, naturally conform to a military type. The towers of St.-Ricquier Abbeville (thirteenth century), Béthune and Comines (fourteenth century) are severe and castle-like in their

THE BELFRY OF VIRE (CALVADOS).

aspect: the windows are small and plain and the towers are loopholed as at Béthune and Comines, and sometimes, as at Béthune (Pas-de-Calais) and Solre-le-Château (Nord), reinforced by turrets corbelled out from the wall. This last feature is sometimes copied in the later belfries, as at Rue (Somme) and Douai and Bergues (Nord). The later towers are, as a rule, taller, more elaborate in design and more richly ornamented, as we should expect in structures that were reared in less troubled and more prosperous days. Thus, Bergues (sixteenth century) has every stage adorned with a panelling of cusped pointed

GISORS (EURE).

ST.-GERMAIN ARGENTAN (ORNE).

RENAISSANCE.

facing p. 234.

arches. Calais (fifteenth and sixteenth centuries) has long panels with blind tracery, and the lofty tower of Arras, which fell before the German guns, presented a highly ornate outline like a late Gothic church steeple, somewhat after the type of that of Antwerp Cathedral.

The Belfry of Évreux.

Upon the towers, in many cases, a lighter superstructure was erected to contain the inevitable carillon of a Flemish town. At Béthune the tower was completed by a slender spire of great elegance, though of somewhat fantastic outline. At Comines the plain and severe tower of the fourteenth century is crowned by a huge bulbous dome, surmounted by an open finial or *flèche* of the seventeenth century,

The Belfry of Bergues (Nord).

and the belfry of Solre-le-Château (Nord) presents a more grotesque appearance, having its tall spire crowned

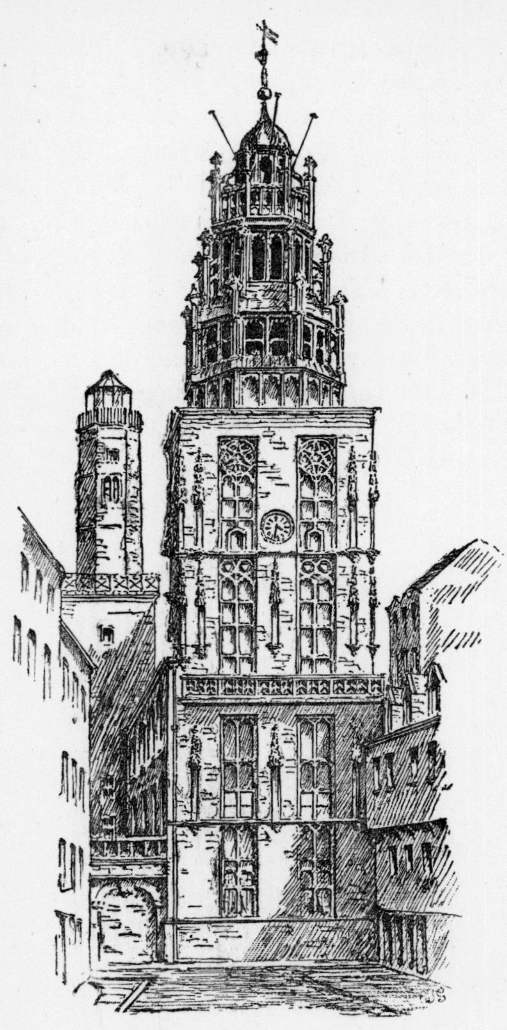

The Belfry of Calais.

by a huge onion-shaped finial, while the four flanking turrets have similar finish of smaller scale. Bergues shows another and pleasing form of domical finish for the carillon stage. A lofty erection of this class with diminutive pinnacles and flying buttresses, and having a flavour of classicalism in its late Gothic design, was added early in the seventeenth century to the square belfry at Calais. It is very effective and stands in a most quaint and picturesque setting, the still more ancient octagonal "Tour-de-Guet" being not many yards distant, and from its carillon the haunting melody of *Gentille Annette* rings out at each hour over the old-world city. The belfries of Évreux, Beaune and Auxerre have upon their stone towers light open spires with pinnacles and flying buttresses, and in conformity with local fashion there are iron cages for bells on the Hôtels-de-Ville of the south, as at Tarascon and Aix-en-Provence.

INDEX I

CHURCHES AND OTHER BUILDINGS REFERRED TO

FRANCE

CALVADOS

EURE-ET-LOIR

FINISTÈRE

GARD

GERS

GIRONDE

HAUT-RHIN

HAUTE-GARONNE

HAUTE-LOIRE

HAUTE-MARNE

HAUTE-SAÔNE

HAUTE-SAVOIE

HAUTE-VIENNE

RHÔNE

SAÔNE-ET-LOIRE

SARTHE

SAVOIE

SEINE

SEINE-ET-MARNE

SEINE-ET-OISE

SEINE-INFÉRIEURE

SOMME

TARN

TARN-ET-GARONNE

VAR

VAUCLUSE

SCOTLAND

IRELAND

BELGIUM

GERMANY AND CENTRAL EUROPE

HOLLAND

ITALY

SPAIN

SWITZERLAND

TURKEY

INDEX II

NAMES AND SUBJECTS

Made and Printed in Great Britain
by Hazell, Watson & Viney Ld.
London and Aylesbury